WELCOME TO FATHERHOOD

The Modern Man's Guide to
Pregnancy, Childbirth, and Fatherhood

David Arrell

Dedication

This book is dedicated to Jennifer, my lovely wife, partner, friend, and source of inspiration. Her endless patience and loving guidance throughout both of our pregnancies and beyond made this book possible. And of course to our lovely children Justin and Dorothy too.

Acknowledgements

Special thanks go out to my good friends David Zeitler and Keith Smith for their helpful edits and suggestions. Additional thanks due to Charlotte Buoni, Mary Anne Smith, Dale Sundermann, Jason Steed, Sara DeSpain, Jim Anderson, Allison Evans, Kirby Monin, Craig Jamison, and Adam & Natalie Ray. This batch of early readers all contributed to ***Welcome To Fatherhood*** in helpful ways.

Table of Contents

ABOUT THIS BOOK & HOW TO USE IT

Congratulations! Just by opening this book and starting to read it you have put yourself in the driver's seat of the most amazing and transformative year of your life. You are going on a journey from being a guy casually hanging out in the Dude Zone to becoming a "guy who just found out he is going to have a kid" to ultimately emerging into the Dad Zone and becoming a full-fledged member of the Fatherhood community. This book is hopefully going to make that adventure so much easier and more fun for you, your pregnant partner, and your eventual new baby.

Many guys inexplicably drag their feet when they find out that they have a baby on the way, and just mumble something along the lines of "I'll figure it out later" when asked about it. This is such a common, yet baffling, reaction to a pregnancy. Like, if their roof got smashed by a hail storm they'd probably get some professional help with it. Or, if they suddenly found out they were being transferred to China for their job they'd probably ask around for advice and read some books. But you hit these guys with "Guess what? We're pregnant!" and they suddenly freeze up and/or imagine they will magically know what to do as that journey unfolds. Those guys are NOT going to do well, and their families will suffer too. But not you! You got this book and are already off to a good start by opening it up to page 1. Like many other areas in your life where you decided that you wanted to do better, you've taken charge of your life here too and are willing to put a little time and effort into making yourself into a stronger version, ready for this next challenge. Good stuff!

My name is David Arrell, and I wrote this book to help out guys just like you. Guys who want to be an awesome supportive teammate for their pregnant partner and an awesome Dad for their new little baby, and are smart enough to realize they could use a little help and guidance along the way. When my wife and I found out we were pregnant with our first child on Thanksgiving in 2015, I was ecstatic! I was 42 years old, on the older side for first-time Dads, and also considered myself to be on the more "progressive" end of the Dad spectrum. My amazing wife Jenn is a Pediatric Nurse Practitioner, so she had the training and experience to really be "in the know" for all things related to babies and infants from the health and development side. I felt like we were all set! As for me, I had just sold my business and was planning on being a 100% "stay home Dad" for the first few years of our kid's life while she continued in her career. I was all-in on all the stuff you'll be hearing about over the next year. I bought and read books on how to prepare for Fatherhood, went to all Jenn's OB appointments, went to 2 different birthing classes, went to various baby supply stores about 50 times, shopped for strollers and car seats, sat through several Doula (pronounced "doolah") interviews, held Jenn's hand through childbirth, cut the cord of our new baby, and happily jumped into the fray of new parenthood by doing my part with feedings, diaper changes, etc... I thought I was doing *ALL* the right things based on what I had read and learned along the way.

And guess what? I still did so, so many things the hard way, or just plain wrong. I made countless mistakes and often felt lost and exasperated along the way. As I blindly fumbled and bumbled my way forward I had countless moments of "Why didn't anybody tell me this?" and "None of those books ever mentioned this obvious situation!" and "I really wish that it didn't take me 17 tries to figure out the best way of doing this task!" I will laughingly tell you about some of my less-than-finer-moments along the way here in this book.

As a result of my experiences (and difficulties), I created and launched the workshop series "***Welcome to Fatherhood***" in May of 2017, 9 months after our son was born. It was designed and built to address precisely those challenging moments I mention above, and to help other Dads-to-be have a smoother journey than I did on their own journeys from "Bump to Baby." The workshop series covered what I felt were the most important elements of the journey from pregnancy to Fatherhood, with equal emphasis placed on being *better connected* to your pregnant partner on *her* journey, and being *better prepared* for Baby and becoming a Dad. I talked to many Dads-to-be, listened to their feedback on the topics covered in the series, and then adjusted my workshop to be both more concise and more impactful.

I then had an opportunity to put my ***WTF*** workshop content directly to the test when my wife and I went through our second pregnancy and childbirth, welcoming our daughter into the world in June of 2018. I did so many things so much better the second time around, yet *still* made plenty of mistakes. I learned tons of new things on how to get *better connected* to Mama and *better prepared* for Baby throughout that pregnancy, childbirth, and homecoming.

That's when I decided to write this book. I've been through 2 pregnancies and childbirths of my own, and coached many other guys through theirs. I've done a lot of things right along the way, and made many, many "mistakes" from which I was able to learn better ways. I've distilled what I've learned into 150 pages of succinct tips, tricks, tools, and techniques to help you *better connect* to Mama on her journey into Motherhood and *better prepare* you for Baby and for your journey into Fatherhood. When Jenn was proofreading ***WTF*** before it came out, she laughed at loud when she finished and said, "Honey, you were a lovely and amazing partner through our first pregnancy, but WHERE THE HELL WAS THIS GUY?!" We both laughed together at how much better I would have been if I had ***WTF*** in my hands back then, and how much easier things would have been for her, and for Baby too.

Lucky for you, you have it in your hands now.

Some basic pointers for you to consider before jumping right into the book: I've organized this book in a chronological fashion, following the normal path from pregnancy to parenthood. While many "Dad books" walk you through this same time frame week by week (and for good reasons which I'll touch on later), this isn't that kind of book. Nor is it just another Boobs-and-Beer "Dad" book with the same lame jokes and scenarios. I am instead more focused on the bigger picture time-frames, the more important stepping-up into Dad Zone opportunities, and helping you get the gist of what things matter most during each phase of the journey. Hence, the book is simply organized to cover Trimesters 1, 2, 3, Labor & Delivery, and then the 4th Trimester back home.

Each chapter begins with a quick overview of that particular leg of the journey, and also a short run through of what to expect from Mama and Baby during this time frame. But then the meat of each chapter is focused on you, or more specifically, focused on giving you helpful and specific tips, tricks, tools, and techniques to *put into practice* so that you are *better connected* to Mama during this transformative time in her life, and *better prepared* for what lies ahead in the next time frame of your journey. These will be presented as **Big Ideas** and **Dad Tips**, both of which will be in **bold** font and numbered sequentially to help you and I keep track of them for future reference. Additionally, these are organized in Appendix A for the **Big Ideas** and Appendix B for the **Dad Tips** at the end of the book for quick and easy reference.

The **Big Ideas** are simply new ideas or ways of thinking that attempt to give you a better sense of the bigger picture reality that you now find yourself in. I believe they will greatly help you better understand the larger context about what is happening now and how you fit into it. Each of the **Big Ideas** connects to and builds upon the previous ones. A good analogy would be to consider them like sequential software upgrades where each "download" helps your thinking see certain things more clearly and therefore function better as you go along. Each chapter also includes **Dad Tips**, which are time-specific actions and/or practical suggestions for you to consider implementing during that particular phase of the journey. These are more numerous but are also mostly just relevant to where you are in the adventure. To illustrate this distinction, imagine you are going on a 5-day adventurous trek through the jungle somewhere. A **Big Idea** would be something like "watch out for the venomous green mamba snake, one bite will kill you" that sort of applies to the whole trek. The **Dad Tips** are more like specific trail tips, like "cross the river right here below the rapids" where it mostly only applies for that specific situation.

Finally, each chapter concludes with two short summary sections, one "For You" and one "For Mama." The "For You" section revisits and wraps up the various **Big Ideas** and **Dad Tips** covered in that chapter. The "For Mama" summary is your secret weapon. It is designed and written for your pregnant partner to read so that she can better understand you and *your* journey here, and helps her get *better connected to you* on it. Many guys have found having their ladies read this last "For Mama" section of each chapter to be the most helpful thing in the whole book! Mainly because it a) somewhat balances out the times she says to you, "here, please read this" while sending you another pregnancy related article, b) it's from another man's perspective, not directly yours, so she'll be more open to hearing things that she may not necessarily like, and c) it shows her that you are interested and involved in this journey to Parenthood that you both are on *together*. All of which encourages her to be *better* *connected* to you too, so please ask your partner to read her "For Mama" summary of each chapter along the way.

I recommend that you read the entire book straight through ASAP in a few dedicated sittings as soon as you get it. C'mon! Its only 150 pages! Don't bother with taking notes, underlining, or anything other than just going through it to get a general sense of how things are going to unfold for you over the next year or so. Doing this quick first read right away will give you HUGE brownie points (or Dad Card credits, a topic we'll cover soon) with Mama, and get you *better connected* to her and her journey. It will also give you a pretty good sense of what to expect over the total course of your journey, regardless of where you are currently, leading to you being *better prepared* for what comes ahead. Reading the whole thing now will also hopefully startle and worry you just enough to get you a bit more focused on wherever you are today, and help you make a few necessary adjustments in your planning for tomorrow.

After this initial quick read through, I then suggest that you go back and slowly reread each individual chapter again as your pregnancy journey begins to head into that chapter's specific timeframe. Read each chapter on this second go around with more attention to the specific tips, tricks, tools, and techniques suggested for the upcoming part of the pregnancy. This time through you can take notes, underline things, or bust out your highlighter. Most importantly, make a point to actually *try* some of the suggested actions mentioned therein! While I put a good amount of effort into helping you get into a better headspace around this adventure with the **Big Ideas** sprinkled throughout the book, ***WTF***'s **Dad Tips** are where the real action lies. They are meant to offer *practical* advice and offer *specific* things for you to do during each stage of your adventure. The sooner you put these things into practice, the easier that journey will be!

I also include 5 of what I call **Scary Moments** too, where we bring the conversation over to the serious side for a minute to talk about possible issues or challenges that might come up, as well as a few do's and don'ts for getting through them stronger together. But don't worry too much about them for now, they are each simply bridges to be crossed when you get to them and will each disappear before the next one comes up.

Please note that in today's world Pregnancy is a medical condition, and since I am not even close to being a Medical Doctor, the content of this book is not intended to substitute for professional medical advice, diagnosis, or treatment. Always seek the advice of your physician or other qualified health care provider with any questions you may have regarding a medical condition.

That being said, it is my hope that you get great value out of this book and that you *put into practice* many of the tips, tricks, tools, and techniques that I offer here. And that hope extends to Mama as well. You are both now in one of the most transformative chapters of your lives here, and like all transformations, there will be challenging and tricky times ahead. ***WTF*** will hopefully help you both have a little easier time, feel a little *better connected* to each other, be a little *better prepared* for what comes next, and have a little more fun along the way too.

Finally, I'll warn you now that my book contains a few curse words here and there. I spent a good chunk of my younger life living and working in Philly and its restaurant scene, which amounts to a double dose of "fuck" as being just an ordinary word that is used all the time in all occasions. I curse much, much less now than I used to, so the few "fucks" and "shits" you'll see are actually only a tiny percentage of my historical range. ☺ And it's no accident that "WTF" is both shorthand for "What the fuck?" and "***Welcome to Fatherhood***."

There is more than a small overlap of those sentiments, as you'll find out soon enough!

Sincere "cheers" to you both!

David

INTRODUCTION

Howdy! Congratulations again on opening this book and jumping right in to your journey to Fatherhood. Did you skip that first section because it looks like instructions, and you're the kind of guy that just jumps in and tries to build it first? Yeah, I get it. THAT'S why I wrote the first section. Head back there and quickly power through it – it will make what I say here a lot easier to follow. Trust me – I wrote this book to be a fast and effective read, but each section builds on the one that came before!

Now that we're all caught up, and assuming that you are a Dad-to-be with a pregnant Mom-to-be in your life, let's get right to the main issue that impacts every couple's pregnancy journey from Day 1 onward. This issue is fundamental to the situation and is not changeable in any way shape or form.

She is pregnant, and you are not.

While this may seem obvious, and will only become more obvious as the months go by and her belly gets bigger, the powerful and significant implications of this reality gap between you two are not obvious at all. You both know that she is on a different trajectory than you right now, and you want to do what you can to be a helpful part of it, right? Well then, let's talk about the same singular sentence that we see pretty much every pregnancy book, article, and website tell us guys when we ask what we can do about it – "Be more helpful and supportive." No matter where we seem to turn for some wisdom or advice, we get that same tired trope thrown at us.

"Be more helpful and supportive!"

I don't think I've ever seen such a saccharine, vague sentiment passed around as legitimate advice anywhere else in my life. Seriously, what the fuck does that actually mean? It's not like all us Dads-to-be are running around being objectively *unhelpful* and *unsupportive*, right? So really, what does that pithy comment actually mean, and why does it seem that that's the basic go-to advice that everybody gives to us Dads-to-be?

Well, first of all, most of those articles and books are written by other women, not guys like me who have actually been in the trenches and lived to tell about it. Second, like we just said a moment ago, it pretty much comes down to the fact that we aren't the ones who are actually pregnant. And we aren't the ones who are going to grow out of our regular body and all our clothes. And we aren't the ones who are expected to push a watermelon-sized Baby out of a lemon-sized hole. So, yeah, there's all that. And unfortunately, there really isn't any direct way to physically assist your pregnant partner with those things. There's also really no way we can ever possibly even begin to understand how any and all of that stuff actually feels either. So, in order to be "helpful and supportive" we stumble about and try to do what we think makes sense-ish, sorta. We go out for random and peculiar food requests, we offer to carry heavy things, we paint the nursery and put together the crib and so forth.

But in spite of all these things we do, and countless others, there remains a fundamental distance and disconnect between Dads-to-be and Moms-to-be. This disconnect is real. When asked by their close friends about how us Dads-to-be are doing, so many pregnant Mamas sort of inhale, look aside, and then sadly mutter something like "well, he's trying, BUT..."

What explains this HUGE disconnect between how us guys think we are doing and how our ladies are actually feeling about it?

Big Idea #1: **Pregnancy turns your lady into an instant Mama.** As it turns out, there is a phrase that quite accurately sums up the typical reality that many couples experience with their first pregnancy and childbirth. "Women become Mothers when they find out that they are pregnant, but men don't become Fathers until the baby is born." The truth behind that phrase is what drives this whole book. This time gap between women becoming Mothers and men becoming Fathers is the ultimate source and cause of the very real disconnect that many couples experience on their first journey from bump to baby. That time gap then snaps shut for many Dads as they stand there in shock holding their brand-new baby - "oh shit, I'm a Dad now, uh, now what?" As I see it, that time gap is pretty much hard-wired into our genes as men and women, which we'll get into in Chapter 1, but there are many hacks we can employ to shrink that gap down quite a bit.

This leads us to our first part of this book's tagline - being *better connected* to Mama on her journey from Maiden to Motherhood, and her feeling *better connected* to you along the way. Some of you guys might be thinking "Well, wait a minute, I'm feeling pretty dialed in over here. My lady and I are totally in sync!" To that I'd say "Great! But how do you think *she* feels about it?" Unfortunately, the vast majority of pregnant women *don't* feel as connected to their partner as they would like to be. And on one hand that's totally expected. As we mentioned above, she actually has a real baby growing inside of her, she is watching her body grow and bulge, she is feeling all kinds of feelings ranging from exhilarating joy to paralyzing anxiety to everywhere in between (often in the same minute). How could you possibly relate to all of that on any meaningful level? **OF COURSE** she is going to have moments of feeling totally all alone out in the wilderness! That's unavoidable to some degree.

However, there are many simple tips, tricks, tools, and techniques that you can use to help bring the two of you closer together in spite of that distance. I'll cover these throughout the book and you'll be able to see the results of putting them to the test for yourself. Your partner may not even be aware of what you are doing half the time, but she'll certainly be thinking about you with a smile on her face when her friends are asking her "so.... how is Baby Dada handling everything with the pregnancy?" when your name comes up. She'll then be smiling even more when she hears about how some of her other pregnant friends feel way less *helped and supported* than she does on their journey because their Dude isn't reading ***WTF*** (yet) and is still prioritizing all of his usual non-baby related Dude Zone interests and hobbies. It also feels pretty awesome when she squeezes your hand and smiles at you while she is telling all your friends and family members how great it is to have such a *helpful and supportive* partner along for the journey.

So, we'll definitely be focused on the *better connected* bit in each and every chapter. And, since most of us guys tend to be more naturally oriented to the *better prepared* side of things, we'll cover lots of ground in that territory also. And not just *better prepared* to become a Father, but *better prepared* for all of the specific challenges you'll face along the way. We'll get you *better prepared* for such things as gift registries, OB/Midwife appointments, car seats and strollers, birth classes, Doulas, birth plans, baby names and many other things you have probably never ever thought about one bit. Don't worry man, I got you covered!

Chapter 1
The Dad Instinct

From Bears and Daggers to Bottles and Diapers

I want you to close your eyes for just a minute and imagine some of the things that you are MOST excited about when you think of becoming a Father. Go ahead, say them out loud to yourself so that they become more definitive ideas and scenarios rather than just vague swirls of thoughts and feelings. Even better would be to make a point to get specific and concrete and write them in the margins here. I know I said earlier not to worry about getting out a pen for the first read through, but go get one now just for this first exercise. Seriously, go get a pen, take a quick minute to think about it, and jot down what comes to mind…

If you're like most guys you probably hit on some of the basics – teaching your kid to fish, or turn a wrench, or riding a bike, or playing catch, or something along those lines. Most of these ideas involve some sort of "wisdom sharing", and possibly connect to something your father or favorite uncle or grandpa shared with you back when you were a kid. And that's awesome. One of the best parts of Fatherhood is indeed having those moments of sharing wisdom and helping your children, boys and girls alike, develop skills and competencies in the world. Ok, now go back and see if you can notice another theme among whatever your specific ideas were that have you most excited. Go ahead, look again.

Here's a hint… how old is your child in these moments? 3 years old? 4? How old does a kid have to be before you can take them fishing?

What about riding a bike? But guess what? Infants don't fish. Or ride bikes. Or do much of anything but sleep, eat, and poop. And cry, sometimes a little, sometimes a lot. There are actually going to be well over 1,000 days and nights before your Baby turns 3. That's a lot of days and nights, and a lot of diapers and bottles too. I'm sure some inspired reader out there might have thought about middle-of-the-night-diaper-changes in their "most excited for" moments, but the vast majority of guys I talk with seem to automatically and unconsciously fast forward to moments that involve their kid being around 3 or 4 years old. Why do you think this is the case??

Well, just imagine jumping in a time machine and going back to ANY TIME in the past from 200 to 200,000 years ago, almost ANYWHERE on the planet, in pretty much ANY culture. Let's now look at where the babies and young children are hanging out and who is taking care of them. I'm pretty sure that what we would mostly see would be extended families of women of various ages and relationships all working together to take care of the infants and young children. Most, if not all, traditional cultures had (and plenty still have, to this very day) clearly defined gender roles and rules, and those roles and rules pretty much kept the men entirely out of the mix when it came to babies and baby rearing. Men weren't merely "not present" for childbirth, breastfeeding, and baby rearing – they were explicitly not allowed! They were kept away from the kids and Mamas and instead sent to go chasing off bears, sharpening daggers, and all the other outward-facing and dangerous things that needed to be done for the community or village.

In fact, only recently have some parts of human culture started to shift to invite and expect men to get more involved in pregnancy, childbirth, and early childhood. Here in the US, male doctors only started being frequently present at childbirth about 100 or so years ago, before then it was all women and Midwifery. The evolution of Dad's role in childbirth and caring for baby have also been constantly evolving and changing as well. When I was born in the early 70's in Chicago my Dad was only allowed to hold me in the hospital for a total of 30 minutes *a day*, and then only during visiting hours and under the direct supervision of one of the nurses. Dads were still flat-out forbidden to be in the delivery room. Up through the 80's and 90's the general cultural expectation also largely still held that Mom would stay in the home and take care of the kids and Dad would go right back off to work. A Dad's role in infant and early child-rearing, while improved from times past, was still severely restricted.

Looking at the historically low to non-existent biological and cultural role for men in pregnancy and child-rearing in this light can be quite revealing. In fact, I see it as creating something akin to a delayed "Dad Instinct" that we inherit from all of our ancestors. This concept can help us get a much better, and more charitable, understanding of the myriad difficulties many modern men are now facing. Put another way, let's stop looking at men's current challenges in getting up to speed on and stepping right into all things baby-related as a character flaw or something else patently negative and unhelpful. Let's instead view men having those challenges as an obvious consequence of cultural norms changing faster and faster, and demanding more meaningful engagement and involvement from us guys several years before our Dad Instincts are really programmed to kick in.

Thankfully, all of those historical cultural frameworks are now being radically reworked and revised, allowing us guys to better appreciate and experience the trials and tribulations of bringing new babies into the world. But until the new norms are figured out and stabilized, our culture's ongoing struggle often makes things more confusing for everybody, Mamas and Dads alike, which brings us right to our next realization.

Big Idea #2: It's a radically different world today for pregnancy, childbirth, and baby rearing. Let all that sink in for moment, it's a pretty big deal. 200,000+ years of doing all things Baby pretty much the same, and then **BOOM**, a massive and radical shift of how society and cultures are organized, with the rate and range of change skyrocketing straight up over the last 100 years. And that hyper-shift is still happening all around us! No wonder so many guys feel a lot of uncertainty and hesitation around what's currently being expected from them, and women too. It's unclear and unprecedented. Being unsure and a little frightened is totally understandable and a natural response to encountering such new and strange territory. Plenty of guys out there take a tentative peek into this murky swamp of uncertainty, do a quick, fearful shudder, and then mumble to themselves "uh... I guess I'll just figure it out when the baby gets here." What a *terrible* plan. A totally understandable reaction, but an absolutely *terrible* plan. You, however, are way ahead of the game by having ***WTF*** in your hands, and you will be even better off after you start to get into it and can try out some of the ideas presented here for yourself.

And guys, let's not forget that these massive shifts are just as disruptive to Mama's cultural inheritance as well, if not even more so. Back in times past women would grow up around lots of other women being pregnant, having babies, breastfeeding, and taking care of infants and children. Multigenerational family groups living together in close proximity created an immersive environment for learning all about child-rearing, almost as if by osmosis. Back then women had more children, on average, and started at younger ages, on average, than they do now. Living in larger extended family groups would tend to create a home life where an average 20-year old pregnant woman would have closely witnessed dozens of pregnancies and childbirths of her mother, sisters, cousins, and aunts and would have grown up constantly pitching in on helping care for other children and babies of the household and neighborhood. She would have grown up constantly surrounded by and assisting with other women's pregnancies and babies, and would have all of these other women around to also help her through her own first pregnancy and her own entry into Motherhood.

That's not the case anymore for the majority of women here in the US in today's modern age. Most women now come from smaller families to start with, live further away from their extended family, and are also waiting until later in life to start a family of their own. Many women are also in the middle of a career path when they first become pregnant, and are surrounded by a choir of different cultural messages on how to manage and juggle families and careers. While all women still have their biological "Mom instincts" intact, the much more important social and culturally provided ones have largely been stripped away. Therefore, your average pregnant woman in today's world is facing way *more* challenging pressures than her foremothers, and has way *less* of a support system to lean on. It's an extremely difficult predicament! And let's not forget the impact of **B1 (Instant Mama)** from the Intro where we discussed women becoming Mothers as soon as they become pregnant, and men not becoming Fathers until the baby is born. Adding that big disconnect with Dad into the vanishing culture of support leaves many a Mama feeling almost entirely all alone in her pregnancy journey. Which is part and parcel of why your lady really needs *you* to start stepping up your Dad Zone game. Now. But how? What does that look like?

Big Idea #3: Dude Zone to Dad Zone, and avoiding the Dud Zones. Up until you find out that you and your partner are going to have a baby you are probably spending a good amount of time hanging out in what I call the Dude Zone. While your relationship with Mama and your job are likely your top two priorities, you also have a bunch of other ones that follow closely behind them. Maybe it's your Fantasy Football league and Friday night darts at the pub with your buddies. Maybe it's online gaming or poker. Maybe it's tinkering with your bike and riding the trails. But it doesn't really matter what it is, it only matters that it's your thing that you like to spend your time, energy, and/or money on and it doesn't involve your job or relationship. All of this is the Dude Zone, and it's good to have a vibrant and healthy life inside of it. Until you find out that you have a baby on the way... Then it's time to step up out of the Dude Zone and start heading towards the Dad Zone.

Making your way to the Dad Zone and earning your official Dad Card isn't a simple, one-time action. The path to the Dad Zone is an ever-evolving series of charges and challenges, with many twists and turns. There's no yellow brick road to find and follow here either, nicely laid out in front of you leading you to success. However, a path does exist ahead for you that is uniquely yours and for you alone to find. There will be a lot of trial and error and bobbing and weaving as you work your way onward and upward to the Dad Zone. As long as you try to stay connected to the bigger picture and do some of the actions discussed in this book to up your Dad Card credits as you go along, then you should succeed. And fortunately for you, I'll also tell you about the two outer boundaries along this course to help you know when you are going astray into danger and to keep you moving in the right direction. These nether regions are called the Dud Zones.

The Dud Zone on the left is Wimpytown. A variety of dudes hang out here but the theme that unites them is that they have all sort of given up on figuring this whole Dad thing out on their own. They sincerely want to be *helpful and supportive,* but defeatedly just wait around for their women to tell them exactly what to do and exactly how to do it. Their internal fire is pretty dim, and they all seem somewhat slouched over and downtrodden. Common phrases heard here include "just tell me what to do," and "I don't have an opinion on it, get whatever you want, dear," and "I don't know, just do it however you like." Many of these guys are seen just stumbling around and muttering *"be helpful and supportive, be helpful and supportive,"* as if they were a bunch of malfunctioning service droids needing to be reprogrammed. They've taken the ideal of selflessness to its terrible extreme, unknowingly ending up almost completely *unhelpful and unsupportive* as a result. Pause for a second, do you really think Mama wants a "partner" that she has to constantly kick in the ass and give specific directions to about everything? Nope. If you catch yourself looking or sounding too much like them, much too often, then reverse your engines and get out of there quick!

The Dud Zone on the right is called Jerkville, and also has an interesting mix of guys hanging around. The common theme that unites them is that they seem overly determined to "stay true to themselves," and "keeping their Man Card," and often appear to be angry and defiant. They'll say things like "well, you're the pregnant one, not me," and "Ugh, I'm not driving all the way across town to get you a smoothie," and "I saw a pregnant zebra fight off two lions on TV last night, surely you can manage to carry a laundry basket up the stairs." These guys have taken the ideal of self-sufficient to the extreme. "You do you, and I'll do me." Again, pause for a second and ask yourself if you think Mama really wants a "partner" that she has to cajole and convince for every single thing? If these characteristics start to routinely manifest in you, then bust a U-turn on the double and head back the other way toward higher ground.

You may find yourself rapidly ricocheting between these two outer Dud Zones from time to time as you struggle to maintain some balance in the middle ground between them or higher ground beyond them. That's absolutely expected, and not just earlier on in the pregnancy, but all throughout the journey as things change and develop. In spite of my best intentions and efforts, I personally spent A LOT of time in these Dud Zones during our first pregnancy. Often, I felt totally disoriented, as if I had one foot in Jerkville and the other in Wimpytown, and I'm certain I said "Either just tell me what you want me to do, or do it yourself" on more than one occasion as my frustrations with trying to find the Dad Zone options boiled over.

These Dud Zone pit stops are pretty common occurrences for the average guy on his way to the Dad Zone, so expect to have your own struggles here. It's tricky trying to *better connect* with Mama in *helpful and supportive* ways while also staying true to your own journey and priorities here. But as long as you keep one eye focused on Mama and her journey and the other one locked on you and yours then you will have nothing to fear, my friend. As the weeks and months go by, you will notice the progress you've made up the hill and further into the Dad Zone. And with ***WTF*** as your trusted guide, you will get *better connected* to Mama along the way and *better prepared* for the challenges ahead.

Chapter 1 Summary for You: Pregnancy and childbirth rules, roles, and expectations for both Mothers and Fathers have changed drastically over the years, and are now extremely different than they were for all of our previous human cultural history. As we discussed in **B1 (Instant Mama)** and **B2 (Different World)**, your main delayed "Dad Instincts" aren't designed to fully kick in until children are perhaps 3 years old, and that big delay isn't going to cut it anymore in today's age. But that's OK. There are a ton of resources out there to help Dads-to-be like you get up to speed (like this book!), and the culture is (slowly) changing for the better in ways to support you. Paternity leave is increasing, Dad books and Dad diaper bags are coming out, baby-wearing is totally cool, and most public men's rooms now have baby changing tables in them. We then covered the Dud Zones in **B3 (Dad Zone)** that you will bounce between on your journey into the Dad Zone. Keep an eye out for the defeated blues of Wimpytown and the angry energies of Jerkville taking hold in you as you undertake your journey. Just try to remember the two basic goals to assist your search for the trail – *better connected, better prepared*. ***WTF*** is just one more tool to help you, your pregnant partner, and your upcoming new baby have an easier time adapting and adjusting to this brave new world. Onward ho!

Chapter 1 Summary for Her: It's a different world today, full of pressures and challenges very different from the preceding 200,000+ years of human cultural history, for both you and your man. Your Mom Instincts probably haven't been fully prepped by years of exposure to large extended families full of pregnancies, babies, breastfeeding, and child-rearing like they would have been in times past, which may lead to you having increased feelings of uncertainty and isolation during your pregnancy. Dad is facing two uphill challenges here. The first is covered in the expression that "Women become Mothers when they find out they are pregnant, and Men become Fathers when the baby is born." While you became immediately busy thinking about extra vitamins and which fish have mercury in them, he is not. He's still the same dude right now, and he's going to struggle a bit as he finds his way to becoming a Dad. The second challenge that complicates things for both of you is that most of his Dad Instincts aren't really programmed to fully kick in until after babies become toddlers and start walking and talking. Today's emphasis on the nuclear family set-up puts a further strain on pregnancy and baby-rearing with both Moms- and Dads-to-be getting bombarded with all sorts of conflicting advice from every direction on every topic from careers to vitamins to baby names to ultrasounds and everything in between. It's a jungle out there! But ***WTF*** is full of tips, tricks, and techniques to help your man jump right in to your pregnancy and into the Dad Zone. It has ideas and tips that will help him get *better connected* to you on your journey from Maiden to Motherhood, and will also help get him *better prepared* for Baby and his jump to Fatherhood. Please be patient with him over this journey, and try to get *better connected* to him and his struggles too. This is all new territory for you both.

Chapter 2
"We're Pregnant!" through The First Trimester

Get Your Head in the Game

"Honey, we're pregnant!!"

So few words, so many implications! Maybe you've been trying to get pregnant for a long time. Or maybe you haven't even thought about it until just this moment. Or maybe, like many couples today, you've been "not not-trying" for some time now. Regardless of your planning, or not, everything in your life just changed due to some version of those magic words. Congratulations!

And also, "Welcome to Fatherhood" to you Dad, because that journey starts now too, even if it doesn't really feel like it's real yet.

This will be a pretty short chapter because there isn't too much for you to do during this 1st Trimester. At least as compared to further on into the pregnancy anyway. ☺ A good analogy is to imagine the pregnancy part of this journey as the beginning portion of a rollercoaster ride. You get buckled in and kind of hang out for a while until the rollercoaster starts slowly moving along the tracks and heads up the first huge hill. Finding out you're pregnant is that first "click" of the seatbelt. "Oh shit, I guess this is really actually happening now." So, you are starting to feel all the butterflies in your stomach, but you also have a good chunk of time to get yourself ready and prepared for what comes next.

However, this particular rollercoaster you're now buckled into actually has an extra-long and slow upward climb to allow you time to get psyched up, which is on purpose because that rush down the other side is going to be indescribably colossal! Therefore, we'll get started by covering some of the basics of what's going on for Mama here so that you can understand her experience and try to *better connect* to it. I'll then jump into some homework for you start working on so that you can get to work on being *better prepared* for what's coming up and aren't just the guy "over there," passively being an outside observer to Mama's pregnancy. But before we get into some specifics of Mama's pregnancy, let's download the next **Big Idea** software upgrade for you.

Big Idea #4: **Her becoming pregnant is the BIGGEST DEAL EVER IN HER WHOLE LIFE up to this point.** HUGE. Way bigger than anything else. Bigger than weddings, funerals, graduations, pretty much anything. You need to just pause for a moment, step back, and really try to understand and appreciate this. Many guys completely fail here. They say things like "Well, that's how we all got here, right?" and "It's not that special, I mean over 4 million babies are born here in the US alone every year, right?" Huge early Dud Zone fail! This approach is completely wrong, even if the information is technically right. Afterall, the same logic applies to dying too, right? Not a big deal until it happens to you. Same with Pregnancy, and especially for Mama.

EVERYTHING in her life will change - physically, mentally, emotionally, spiritually, etc. - and it's up to you to try to track and support those changes. Remember that whole *helpful and supportive* bit? The bad news (for you) is that many of those changes for her will be slow-moving and completely invisible. You'll only be able to directly see and witness her growing belly and changing wardrobe. Like shifting tectonic plates, those deeper and more impactful changes are going to be largely invisible, yet still present a whole host of challenges for you to figure out and navigate. And you're pretty much going to have to do that mostly on your own.

WTF, and any other particular "Dad book" out there, can only offer up so much general advice. It's up to you to actually pay close attention to Mama and put the work in to remain somewhat on pace with her transformation into Motherhood. The good news (for you) is that there is *nobody* that she would rather go on this journey with than you. You are #1 in her eyes here and you really don't have to do too much (for now) to remain there and be totally on point as *her* man, especially as compared to some of her friends' dudes who are just going to "wing it and figure it out once the baby gets here." Those dudes are fucked. That's like waiting until after you've already stepped out of the airplane to figure out how to put on your parachute. Too late now, yo! But not you, you're on point and in the game. Way to go getting involved right away and doing your part to get *better connected* to her and *better prepared* for the journey ahead.

Big Idea #5: **Mama may be feeling, and expressing, a *ton* of ANXIETY right now.** This is natural and completely understandable. It follows from her parts of **B1 (Instant Mama)**, **B2 (Different World)** and **B4 (Biggest Deal).** She will experience A LOT of strong hormones kicking in, intense feelings, mood swings, and every emotion you never even knew was a thing. However, the most important thing for you to recognize is that underneath the surface there may be lots, and lots, and lots of **ANXIETY** pushing this all up to the forefront. Is the baby OK? Am I eating right? Am I going to be a good Mom? What am I going to do about my job? Is he (you) going to be a great Dad? Is the baby OK? This list goes on and on and round and round. Again, totally normal and completely understandable. BUT, anxiety is an absolutely terrible thing to try to manage alone. It's also what I call a "pusher," in that anxiety often feels like a tremendous pressure pushing people to "Do something! Anything! Don't just sit there!" So, just a head's up here, that "push" energy is going to be coming at you, fast and strong!

This tremendous pressure of pregnancy anxiety can absolutely cause both you and Mama tremendous grief, but only if you let it. Fortunately, there are a few simple things you can do to help you both cruise through these potentially rough waters with only the slightest bit of rockiness. We'll jump into those right away after going through a quick overview of the pregnancy journey and the changes you can expect to see and experience.

The general time frame from conception to Baby's birth is about 40 weeks, and this overall period is commonly divided into 3 trimesters. Baby's gestational age is measured and tracked in weeks. The 1st Trimester covers everything up through week 12, the 2nd includes weeks 13 – 28, and the 3rd is from week 29 – birth. Pregnancy terms are divided this way for reasons we'll get into later, but for now this is how most people generally break up the 9-month-ish gestation period. Therefore, as mentioned earlier, we'll follow that 3 trimester timeline for how we discuss the pregnancy journey and get into the things you need to be thinking about and doing as each trimester approaches and unfolds.

After finding out you are expecting a baby, one of the first things that should happen next here in the 1st Trimester is to schedule an appointment with Mama's Midwife or Obstetrician (OB). This first visit can cover any number of things but the main goals are to 1) confirm and date the pregnancy, 2) arrive at an *estimated due date* (more on this later), and 3) collect some medical and family history from you both to help determine what additional testing might be recommended. This first visit often happens between weeks 6 and 8 of the pregnancy, and you'll then also probably schedule a follow up visit for around 12 – 14 weeks as you enter the 2nd Trimester. Oh, and yes, you ABSOLUTELY need to *happily and willingly* go to ALL of her

Midwife/OB appointments! Remembering **B4 (Biggest Deal)** and **B5 (Anxiety)**, what may seem to be just regular and routine check-ups to you are super important and perhaps even a bit scary for Mama. You need to be there at these appointments as both Mama's partner and as Baby's Dad in order to stay current on what's going on with them both, routine as these may feel to be. Remember, the goals here are to be *better connected* to Mama, and *better prepared* for what lies ahead.

The 1st Trimester time period is also where we come across the first of what I'm going to call the **Scary Moments**. As mentioned back at the beginning of ***WTF***, there are 5 **Scary Moments** that I'll address, and these are specific times when something might "go wrong" in a way that may have a severe impact on you, Mama, and Baby. While most of this book is written in somewhat of a jokey, guy-language tone, these **Scary Moments** are the times when we need to get serious for a minute and take the conversation over to "The Real," as my buddies and I say. No time for joking here, so please turn the music down and listen up for a minute when we get to them.

Scary Moment #1: This 1st Trimester is the time period when there is the greatest risk for a miscarriage. A miscarriage is when the pregnancy spontaneously self-terminates, and most of the time the actual cause is unknown. They happen much more frequently than most people realize, in fact, there is a 15% chance of miscarriage occurrence for all women. Miscarriage risk is the highest during the first 6 – 8 weeks, but the chances of one happening significantly drop after the 12th week. Therefore, many couples choose to wait until after 12 weeks before publicly announcing their pregnancy to their larger circle of family, friends, and coworkers. Due to its relatively common occurrence and huge emotional impact, miscarriage is a topic that you and Mama should definitely sit down and discuss as soon as possible, if even only briefly. Miscarriage used to be one of those "taboo topics" that was only whispered about behind closed doors, but fortunately the larger culture is turning and it is now a much more open and accessible topic and experience to be shared.

You should feel free to initiate this conversation with Mama, and it could start with something like "Hey Babe, I was reading up on pregnancy stuff the other day and came across the topic of Miscarriage. I had no idea how common that was, can we talk about it for just a few minutes? I want to hear your thoughts about it." Your chat with her should then touch upon the following topics at some point:

- Miscarriage affects 15% of women, which is about 1 in 7, so it isn't an uncommon experience. Ask if she knows of any friends or family members that have gone through one. How did they process those strong feelings?
- Most men tend to react to a miscarried pregnancy with something like "that's ok honey, we can try again." Remembering **B1 (Instant Mama)**, for many men a "lost pregnancy" is not that big of a deal and is just a minor speed bump, something you simply acknowledge for a moment before moving on. Remembering **B4 (Biggest Deal)** THIS IS NOT THE CASE FOR MOST WOMEN. You might have lost a pregnancy, but she just lost *her baby*. That's a big difference. Ask her to share her thoughts and fears about it and then keep your mouth shut and JUST LISTEN empathetically.
- Remind her that you are both doing the very best you can right now to take care of Baby, and that some people say that a miscarriage is just Nature's way of recognizing that things just weren't working out this time, but then *never* mention that thought again! In the event of a miscarriage your partner will likely experience this as a profound loss. It will probably be an intense experience, and likely cause a certain degree of reflection/blame/guilt. "Was it my fault? What could I have done differently? Will it happen again?" These are real and

deep emotions and she deserves the understanding and emotional space she needs to grieve what is experienced as a profound loss to her.

- Tell her that in the unlikely event that you do have a miscarriage that you will NOT TRY TO RUSH HER INTO ANOTHER PREGNANCY or talk about "trying again next month." You'll just be super chill, patient, and extra *helpful and supportive* here.

There are a lot of great additional resources on the ***WTF*** website and elsewhere for ideas and advice on how to consider the impact and implications of a miscarriage if it happens, so it's not the worst idea for you to independently do a little research on the topic ahead of time in the spirit of getting *better prepared*. Please look further into those sources of help and comfort in the event that you and Mama have that happen to you, and whatever else you do or decide, commit to being gentle with each other in the aftermath.

Ok, enough of the scary miscarriage talk, and there are plenty of much better resources than me on the topic out there should you need them, so let's move on.

As for little Baby, in the 1st Trimester they will grow from the size of a poppy seed (.05 inches) to the size of a C-battery (2.1 inches) by week 12. Mama is using her energy to help Baby get their new home in her belly ready by helping build up the amniotic sac, placenta, and umbilical cord. Baby is also hard at work growing and constructing all the basic building blocks of becoming a little human, including all the internal organs, heart, brain, and even teeth. Fun fact, if Baby is a girl then all of her eggs (your future grandkids) are being formed now too! At 10 weeks Baby goes from being an embryo to a fetus, and by 12 weeks begins to develop reflexes, like thumb-sucking, and even has their cute little face mostly formed, just in time for the 12-week ultrasound appointment.

As for Mama and what she is experiencing, this 1st Trimester is where almost all of the morning sickness happens due to the strong pregnancy hormones kicking in. In addition to morning nausea, the 1st Trimester is often marked by some *interesting* food reactions, especially the smells of certain foods. Here's a funny example. Before and then during my wife's first pregnancy we would often walk up to a neighborhood ice cream shop in the evenings after dinner for a tasty treat. The usual route would take us right past this yummy little café that was famous for its curry fries, so much so that they would keep their doors open almost all the time just to have that delicious smell waft out onto the street. Our "usual route" was dramatically changed one evening when we walked by on our way to the ice cream shop, as we had many, many times before, and my smile at the curry smell was suddenly interrupted by the sound of my wife retching in the bushes screaming about "those horrible fucking curry fries!!" Guess what? We didn't walk that particular route ever again the rest of the pregnancy, and she never did bounce back to her pre-pregnancy enjoyment of that place either. So, don't be surprised if her preferences for certain foods and smells radically changes. Just roll with it and eat your curry fries on your own time. ☺

A few other changes to be watchful for – tender and enlarged breasts, constipation, increased urination, and fatigue. Don't be surprised if your old habits of "Netflix and chill..." turn into "Netflix and she's asleep on my arm and now it's really cramping and it's not even 8pm yet?! WTF?!"

Now that we have covered both Mama's and Baby's situations here, let's cut back over to you, our fearless Hero. As mentioned earlier, there really isn't all that much for you to actually do here in the 1st Trimester. However, there are a few things simple ways to slightly change your behavior and language around the pregnancy that will pay big dividends in the *better connected* and *better prepared* departments as time goes by. We'll cover them in the following section of **Dad Tips** for the 1st Trimester – How to get your head in the game now to better set yourself up for success later:

Dad Tip #1: **Keep the Big Ideas mentioned above in mind *at all times* as you chart your course forward.** In fact, it's probably a good idea to read over them once a week as reminders for what she's going through, and here they are again. **B1(Instant Mama)** is that women become Mothers right away, **B2(Different World)** is that it's a different world today than the past, **B4(Biggest Deal)** is that this pregnancy is her biggest deal ever, and **B5(Anxiety)** is the power and push of anxiety. She's already plugged into the "Mom Space" but is probably struggling a bit to whatever degree she feels unprepared and disconnected from her instincts. You're being called into Dad duty about 3 years before *your* cultural instincts are programmed to kick in, so now you're both in over your heads. Awesome, right?

As covered in **B3 (Dad Zone)**, your job in this first Trimester is to start moving out of the Dude Zone and begin making your way towards the Dad Zone, using your frequent forays into the Dud Zones of Wimpytown and Jerkville as guard rails to redirect you back along the way. The most common challenges for Mama in this phase are nausea and anxiety, and a big part of your role here is helping her manage both of them. Being mindful of these 5 **Big Ideas** makes all the difference for both you and Mama if and when stress starts creeping into things. Deep breaths, and lots of patience for both her and yourself, you got this.

Dad Tip #2: Know how many weeks pregnant she is *at all times*. This is a big one. *Better connect* with her by getting on track with the progress of the pregnancy and in sync with what's happening with the baby right away. I earlier mentioned that one of the things that will come out of the first Midwife or OB appointment is a good grasp of the age of the pregnancy as measured in weeks. Even if you are certain of the exact date that you kicked off this pregnancy, they will still do some funny math and calculations based on previous period times and whatnot, so don't get too bogged down by this aspect. The takeaway is that ALL pregnancies are tracked in weeks, not months! Everybody in the know will ALWAYS talk about pregnancies in weeks. Months will only be occasionally used as shorthand in casual conversations. Pregnancies are medically tracked this way because Baby's growth and developmental milestones are more accurately marked and measured in weeks. For example, you'll be able to hear your baby's heartbeat around 9 weeks, they'll start to suck their thumbs at 16 weeks, you can feel them hiccupping at 25 weeks, etc...

Now, go into your calendar or calendar app and mark ahead *all* Baby's age weeks from this week till 2 weeks past the estimated due date. Your OB will have told you more or less what day of the week your "week age" changes so go ahead and mark down all the week ages for the next 30+ Mondays, or whatever day of the week you and Mama choose. Make a point to mention this number to Mama each week as it changes to show her that you're tracking the pregnancy's progress too. Remember this number and bring it up in conversation with friends, or better yet, YOU answer when somebody asks you guys how far along you are in the pregnancy. Huge Dad Card credits to the guys out there that can regularly answer this question. You'd be amazed to know that it's probably less than 10 percent of all Dads-to-be.

As a further part of this plan, it's a great idea for you and your partner to get a pregnancy tracking app, such as Ovia or What To Expect When You're Expecting (don't worry, she already has them) and make it a weekly "date" to sit down together to watch the short 5-minute videos that give you all the updates on what's happening with the baby's growth and development each week along the way. They're pretty funny and informative, and often give Baby's size in terms of funny objects like fruits and animals. Telling your friends that growing Baby is now the size of a chipmunk or hedgehog always gets a laugh.

Pro tip: Offer to help document her progress by taking a "baby bump pic" around the same time each week. She probably won't be obviously pregnant for a little while yet, but keeping a file of weekly "bump pics" is a great way to help you *better connect* with your partner and also help you remember what week of the pregnancy you are in. Doing these few simple things couldn't be any easier and will pay awesome dividends in your partner's appreciation of your involvement in the pregnancy – *helpful and supportive* indeed!

Dad Tip #3: Ask her on the daily about how she is feeling today, and then ask her *separately* how Baby is doing as you affectionately put your hand on her belly. Asking these as separate questions early on, and then continuing to do so as the pregnancy progresses, is a great way to show her that you still see her as *her*, and care about her as *her*, as her own person separate and above Baby and pregnancy. And asking about Baby separately shows her that the baby is a real person for you, not just an "it", with their own thing going on and that you are thinking about them that way. Winning!

We'll wrap up this chapter by getting into another **Big Idea** which I refer to as "Mom Comms." They will be a great tool you can use to "hack" your relationship a bit, and apply to various situations that come up with specific actions and plans to intentionally make things easier for both you and Mama. Strategic use of these "Mom Comms" is going to be a great "go to" move for to you to use time and time again to *better connect* with your partner and *better prepare* you for the road ahead.

Big Idea #6: **"Mom Comms", and the "Love Languages" in action.** We'll talk a lot about "Mom Comms" throughout the book, so it's important that you get a good grasp of them here. Generally speaking, "Mom Comms" are communication tools to help you do and phrase certain things the best way possible so that she feels *better connected* to you on this journey, and to help you keep your Man Card alive and well at the same time you are building up your Dad Card credits. Win-win situations are our ideal outcomes here. For simplicity's sake I will refer to your Man Card when talking about actions that prioritize you taking care of yourself (but safely out of the Dud Zone of Jerkville), and Dad Card for those that show you are putting your family first (but not falling into the Dud Zone of Wimpytown). These are perhaps outdated and silly phrases, but they do a good job of covering some (at times) competing needs. I'll reference them quite a bit throughout the book, and even throw in a *$ka-ching$* here and there to emphasize the "credits" you can earn on them at specific times. FYI, the Dad Zone concept we hit on in **B3(Dad Zone)** requires an equal amount of both Man Card and Dad Card credits to get in, so try to plan your actions to earn them equally. Win-win, *$Ka-ching$!*

For starters, some of you might have heard of Gary Chapman's book, "The 5 Love Languages." It's one I definitely recommend that all couples read so that they can better communicate their love for each other in ways that are best understood and felt by their partners. Most people find that they REALLY appreciate it when their partners do things primarily along 1 or 2 of these "languages", and the remaining ones, while nice, don't really feel quite as impactful. I'll recap the 5 Love Languages here for you briefly and give you a few examples of what that might look like if you were to start to put them into practice here early in the pregnancy adventure. While they are all pretty self-explanatory, they are also very helpful in identifying a million simple little things that you can do or say that have huge impacts. **Your goal here is to identify Mama's top 2 Love Languages and then spend 90% of your Love Language efforts in those categories.** Important caveat, you don't actually need to increase your total efforts in Love Language output, but knowing her favorites will just help you be smarter about how you spend your energy here.

1. **Acts of Service** – Think of any task or chore that is slightly uncomfortable for somebody (somebody like your pregnant partner) that is fatigued, bloated, and starting to feel like a stranger in their own body. Now find ways to do some of those uncomfortable things for her. Easy examples can include taking her car to the car wash for her and filling up the gas tank, emptying the dishwasher after she goes to bed again at 7:30pm, picking a different show to watch by yourself rather than plowing right ahead into the show you used to watch together before she starting going to bed at 7:30 every night. See? Easy stuff! But for people who "hear" the Love Language of Acts of Service each of these things will be met with a "wow, thanks, I really appreciate that you did that!"
2. **Words of Affirmation** – This is a big one for pregnant ladies, even if it's not normally one of their top Love Languages. Remember **B5 (Anxiety)** about your partner's likely anxiety about the baby, her life, and her body's transformation. Your kind and loving Words of Affirmation can be like water in the desert for her soul. Some examples include "you're doing such a good job thinking about Baby with your _____ (food choices, vitamin choices, cleaning products, etc.…), thank you honey!", "You wear your pregnancy so well, you're absolutely radiant and beautiful", "I know you're thinking about Baby all the time, he/she/they are so lucky that they are going to have you for a Mom!" Pretty much any acknowledgement you can find that touches upon a) that she's going to be a great Mom, b) she's doing a great job taking care of the baby already, and/or c) that you think she is more beautiful than ever are all good things here. Even if you are totally being cheesy and she knows that you are just buttering her up before you go to the bar and catch the game with your buddies, she'll still smile at

these things and feel all warm and cozy inside if this is one of her favorite love languages.

3. **Physical Touch** – This one can be tricky, because many of us guys are used to physical touch often leading to, uh, more "physical activity." That's what ultimately got us into this situation in the first place, right? However, Physical Touch in this context is much more of the non-sexual kind. Hand holding, shoulder squeezing, LOTS of spontaneous hugs (paired with some Words of Affirmation), a hand on a leg while in the car, so on and so forth. While some women report increased sexual desire while pregnant, other women report a significant *decrease* in sexual desire, especially as their body grows larger and more uncomfortable. That's cool man, this is preparing you for about the first 6 months after the baby comes when she will likely have ZERO sexual desire. Don't take it personally, just understand that this is how things will likely shake out. In the meantime, lots of gentle touches throughout the day are money in the bank for Dad Card credits that you might need to cash in later in the "Mom Comms" department.
4. **Gifts** – The smaller the better here, counterintuitively. Flowers from the grocery store, a simple card with a few sentences written therein (words of affirmation), a scarf (soft, and in her favorite color), a cute pair of baby shoes, anything that seems spontaneous and just shows her that you were thinking of her (and/or Baby) will do just fine here. Remember, if this is one of her Love Languages then the functional utility of the gift is almost irrelevant, it's the fact that you thought of her and got her a small gift, that's the big impact here. The more spontaneous, the better!
5. **Quality Time** – Another one that can be harder for some guys to really connect with, but that can make a huge impact on your relationship now. Quality Time that is baby-focused is a good two-for-one move here. Some examples include going to

look at crib options, starting a rough draft of the baby registry (yes, that's a thing, and yes, we'll cover that later), looking up name options and tracking trends in name popularity over time, sitting down with her and 100% focusing on your weekly baby update videos, etc.... Just try to think of something that you have NEVER had a single thought EVER about doing as a non-Dad-to-be - that should give you plenty of ideas.

These short summaries may have given you enough to go on to figure out which are Mama's favorites, but if not, it's totally fine to sit down with her and ask her what are her preferred methods of feeling into your love for her. Better yet would be to go for some easy *better connected* Dad Card credits here and sit down together to take some of the easy online tests out there. You can also clarify your preferred methods for feeling into her love for you here, but that's not really the main point right now. These Love Languages can be a useful neutral 3rd party to reference on occasion if and when you're feeling disconnected from each other. Most importantly, these Love Languages are a great win-win tool for you to put to use early and often in the pregnancy. They help you guys stay *better connected* on the journey and *better prepare* you for the rougher waters ahead once Baby gets here.

Let's wrap up this chapter by playing with a quick hypothetical example here from our second pregnancy so you can see the "Mom Comms" and Love Languages in action. One Sunday morning during our 2nd pregnancy I noticed that Jenn seemed a little extra down and withdrawn. I started off by asking "Hey babe, are you feeling OK, you seem a little down this morning?" She paused, longer than a second, and then said, "Oh, it's nothing, I'm just feeling a little tired." I didn't quite believe that was the whole truth, but I didn't want to continue to ask and badger her about it since I respect her space and autonomy. I then remembered I was having some friends over later that afternoon to watch the Eagles-Cowboys game. I wanted to be *helpful and supportive* in supporting her pregnancy journey, especially the harder parts, but what does that look like here?

Dud Zones Alert! I didn't want to miss left and end up in Wimpytown by simply offering to cancel my plans because she wasn't feeling well for some reason. And I didn't want to miss right and go to Jerkville and say something like, "well, now's your chance to talk to me about it. Kick-off is at 1, and I'm not gonna be able to help you with whatever you got going on once the game starts." I also didn't want to just shrug my shoulders and simply do nothing, not at the cost of her maybe still feeling all weird and perhaps even emotionally abandoned while I'm over there happily eating chips and yelling at the refs with my buddies once the game comes on. What to do?

"Mom Comms" and Love Language time, *$ka-ching$!* Knowing her two favorite Love Languages are Acts of Service and Gifts, I quickly devised a plan to try to *better connect* with her and *better prepare* for my afternoon. "Honey, I'm going to run out to the hardware store to grab something, I'll be back in about 45 min" I said as I headed for the door. Indeed, I did go to the hardware store to grab something for my weekend project, but more importantly on the way home I stopped by her favorite local café and got her a yummy bacon, egg, & cheese breakfast sandwich, a donut, and her usual latte (decaf now though). I walked in the door and immediately gave her a big hug. I then gently took her hands and said "I can't imagine how tough it is being pregnant, but I'm pretty sure you're doing a great job. And I'm also pretty sure that bacon and donuts might make things just a tiny bit better." I then gave her the bag of treats and her drink, a kiss on the forehead, and headed out to the garage to work on my project for a bit. *$Ka-ching$!!* Money in the bank for my Dad Card.

Later on, about an hour before my buddies were coming over, I said "Babe, the Eagles game starts in about an hour, is there anything you'd like help with until then?" Whether she had something in mind or not, I certainly paved the way for earning some Man Card credits and enjoying a fun afternoon of friends and football. She felt *better connected* to good ol' *helpful and supportive* me, I avoided the Dud Zones and earned some Dad Card and Man Card credits along the way. Win-win, *$ka-ching$!*

Chapter 2 Summary for You: This chapter was about getting your head in the game and building a better understanding of what's happening now, especially as regards pregnant Mama and her experience. As we covered in **B4 (Biggest Deal)**, becoming pregnant is the biggest thing EVER for her. This fact, plus all the pregnancy hormones, may cause Mama to have a lot of anxiety about pretty much anything, but mostly focused on the baby growing inside of her as touched on in **B5 (Anxiety)**. Your best way of being a *helpful and supportive* partner to her through this 1st Trimester is to first understand these things, and to then be patient with her and her way of adjusting to her new reality as mentioned **D1 (Big 4 Ideas)**. We also briefly covered the risks and impact of a miscarriage to help you better prepare for that possibility in **Scary Moment #1**. You can help her feel *better connected* to you on this journey by making time to sit with her each week and watch the Baby Development videos, and just as important, follow the **D2 (Weeks)** advice and be up to speed on what week of pregnancy you are in at all times by checking your calendar as often as needed to remind you. **D3 (Separate)** covered asking how she and Baby are doing as separate questions as a great way to show her you care, but your Golden Ticket to success in earning Dad Card credits from this point forward is to really double down on your efforts to *better connect* to her by utilizing Mom Comms and her preferred Love Languages as discussed in **B6 (Mom Comms).** These efforts will also pay off for you by creating space for you to keep your Man Card credits going and still pursue your interests and hobbies, whatever they may be (golf, dart league, wood shop, whatever) ... except video games. Tread very carefully with the video games. For some reason even the most awesome pregnant

Mamas can be driven to fury when they see their non-pregnant partners playing video games. Sorry dudes, but firing up the Xbox may be an immediate penalty cash out of whatever Love Language Dad Card credits you may have accrued.

Chapter 2 Summary for Mama: You have officially embarked on the single biggest transformational journey of your entire life, going from Maidenhood to Motherhood. Your man, however, has probably not budged even an iota out of the Dude Zone. At least not yet. No matter how hard he tries, Dad could never possibly understand what you are going through from this point forward. However, he loves you very much and really does want to help you have an easier time with everything. Please be patient with him and put your energy into finding *specific* ways for him to be *helpful and supportive*.

Directly ask him for simple things to make your life easier, such as to help you by carrying your laundry up the stairs for you, or to skip your usual Saturday brunch spot for a few weeks because the smell of all that cooking makes your stomach turn. Keep your requests *specific and simple* for now. Watching your weekly *What To Expect When You're Expecting* videos together with him is a great idea, as is making a point of encouraging Dad to still go to the bar with his friends occasionally, even if you don't feel like going.

Remember, you may be pregnant and not feeling well, but he is still his same ol' self. With help from you and ***WTF*** his Dad Zone instincts will start to kick in eventually, just not right away, and it's important to you both to try to understand each other's version of this journey and be supportive of it. You are still two separate people having two separate journeys through pregnancy right now. And while separate for now, there are plenty of moments ahead where they will start to weave more closely together before fully intertwining when Baby gets here and you become new parents together. Try to be patient with his slow movements out of the Dude Zone and into the Dad Zone and don't try to poke, prod, and push him along too hard just quite yet.

Chapter 3
The 2nd Trimester

Setting the Table

We used the phrase "get your head in the game" to cover the 1st Trimester, so let's switch metaphors again and go over to "setting the table" to cover this one. Your special dinner guest will be arriving in just a few more months, so now is the time to stop just thinking about it all and to start actively planning for what you're going to need when your whole world changes. The good news for both you and Mama is that you are now entering the window that is considered by many to be the "easiest" part of your pregnancy. The 2nd Trimester covers weeks 13 – 28 and is still the part of the roller coaster ride where you are just click-click-clicking your way up the hill and are enjoying the view from the increasing height.

Depending on how far into the 1st Trimester you were when you found out you were pregnant, you've probably settled down into your seat somewhat, and the top of the hill is still pretty far away. You might have an occasional flash of nervousness about what lies ahead, but for the most part this leg of the journey is often a pretty enjoyable experience. Whatever morning sickness Mama might have experienced is usually coming to an end, and her energy reserves should also be returning to near her previous levels. Quick tip - now is a great time for the two of you to figure out a healthy new hobby that you can enjoy together from here to Baby and beyond. Pub Night at Paddy's just isn't gonna cut it anymore.

Baby is growing more quickly now too, and you'll probably have another routine ultrasound appointment scheduled for some time around the 20th week or so, at which time your OB should be able to identify the sex of your baby. The 2nd Trimester kick-off is also when many couples go "fully public" with announcing the pregnancy to their larger network of friends and extended family. A common thing is to put some sort of stylized cute pic up on all your social network pages, but before we get deeper into these things and the overview of Mama and Baby, let's go right into the next Big Idea concerning where you are right now – the "Birth Space".

Big Idea #7: Understanding the "Birth Space" concept will *greatly* improve your experience of the next 9 months, and Mama's too. As we covered in **D3 (Dad Zone),** you should be saying your final good byes to the Dude Zone by now. This new concept of the Birth Space is a good way to understand the strange land in which you now find yourself, and through which you will pass on your way to the Dad Zone. The challenges you'll face ahead will probably lead you to bounce in out of the Dud Zones of Wimpytown and Jerkville on occasion, and that's perfectly fine as long as you don't spend too much time hanging out in there. I've found that its helpful to think of this journey through the Birth Space as akin to traveling to a foreign land, a land that has its own language, customs, and other unique cultural and physical artifacts. This land is very peculiar indeed and will absolutely baffle those that are unprepared for both its utter strangeness and its undefined time period.
Once you go public with the pregnancy here at the beginning of the 2nd Trimester is when the Birth Space and its inherent weirdness really starts to take over. There are all kinds of new photography considerations, from bump pics to announcement pics to ultrasound pics (3D, 4D, 5D?) to birth photographer angles that bring in whole new definitions of the term "head shot." Then you have the perplexing array of words and concepts that you've never even heard before, much less been forced to make intelligent-ish decisions about.

Doulas, diapers, breast pumps, fundal height, baby AI implants (just kidding, mostly), and who knows what else. It's a weird land full of weird stuff, and you don't get to just be a passive tourist here, unfortunately. But don't worry too much, ***WTF*** is your trusted guide here. With it in hand and the help of a few key allies, you should make it through to the Dad Zone without too much unnecessary drama. Drama, yes. Unnecessary drama, no.

Back to Mama's journey again, she will continue to have lots of bodily changes during this 3-month timeframe, most notably enlarging breasts, thickening hair, and that "healthy glow" of pregnancy on her face. She will also start to more visibly show her pregnancy bump as these weeks go by. On the more unpleasant side, many women report a variety of other symptoms now such as increased headaches, back aches, frequent urination, hemorrhoids, varicose veins, congestion, and nosebleeds. Fun stuff, eh? However, overall most women really start to get comfortably settled into their pregnancy by now since the risk of miscarriage from this point on is extremely low and their unpleasant morning sickness symptoms have disappeared. They are finally are able to relax a little bit deeper into the process and start to enjoy the journey more.

As for Baby, both their growth and development are really kicking into a higher gear now and going through the 2nd Trimester. While they begin this period at just under 3 inches long and weigh less than an ounce, they will be almost 15 inches long by the end of it and measure nearly 2 pounds. They can start to hear sounds by week 18 and will recognize Mama's voice by week 25. Most of the time you'll be able to find out Baby's sex at the regularly scheduled 20-week ultrasound (more on that later), and Mama will be able to feel Baby's hiccups and other movements by then too!

This 2nd Trimester timeframe also includes your and Mama's two biggest outward-facing and general public-focused moments of the pregnancy part of the journey. The first unique thing to consider here at the very beginning of the 2nd Trimester, and what plunges you deeper into the Birth Space is the "official" pregnancy announcement situation. As I mentioned earlier, due to miscarriage concerns many couples wait until after week 12 to go public with the big announcement and no longer keep the pregnancy news confined to just the small circle of family and friends that you brought on board right away. Whenever and however you decide to open up that circle, there are a few things to keep in mind.

While some couples go all out and get a professional photographer for the official pregnancy announcement, most take a pretty low-key approach and do something like post a pic of baby-sized sneakers next to pairs of their own shoes and say something like "Baby Smith will be joining us in August!" This is another chance for you to *better connect* to Mama and offer some helpful input on how to go about doing it in a way that you feel best fits your style as a couple. Maybe you guys are Chuck Taylor All-Star types? Maybe Ballroom dancers? Maybe you have an awesome dog who is now going to be a "big brother"? You most likely have only paid a small amount of attention, if any, to your various friends' and family's baby announcements in the past, but a quick internet search should give you a good idea of the range of options out there. At the end of the day, go with whatever your pregnant partner wants to do to, keeping your attention on the bigger picture goal of feeling *better connected* to each other.

Remember **B4 (Biggest Deal)**, that this pregnancy is absolutely the biggest deal ever for her, bigger than her wedding and everything else. Try to keep this fact in mind, along with your goal of being *better connected* to her experience of things, if she does in fact bring up the idea of getting professional pregnancy pictures. A few hundred bucks might be worth it for her to feel happy about it, and will definitely get you big Dad Card credits in the being *helpful and supportive* department. And just think what a bargain a few hundred bucks is when compared to wedding photo prices these days!

The other big "public" thing here in the 2nd Trimester happens a bit later on, right after the 20-week ultrasound appointment, which brings us to our next Scary Moment.

Scary Moment #2: The 20-week ultrasound appointment. For many couples this appointment can be the most nerve-wracking part of the entire 2nd Trimester. It includes a basic anatomy scan to determine if everything "looks right" with Baby, as well as additional opportunities for genetic testing and screening. You may recall having conversations with your Midwife or OB much earlier in the pregnancy to get the health histories of both you and Mama, as well as family genetic conditions too. While most genetic concerns may have been cleared up with earlier visits, this 20-week ultrasound is when the OB can get a much better look at Baby to make sure all the organs are present, in the right places, and appear to be working correctly. Many couples, and especially Mamas, report feeling both very high excitement and anxiety as this appointment comes up. Is Baby Ok? Does everything look right? Do any of the family health history concerns show up?

All of these thoughts and questions can be very anxiety inducing and stressful, mainly for Mama, but for you too. Understand this process and expect to feel both nervous and excited heading into your appointment. It will last over an hour, and most places forbid the technicians doing the scan to tell you anything other than the sex of the baby, especially if there is anything that needs a closer look by the OB or Midwife. After the scan is complete the Midwife or OB will look at the results in their office privately before discussing them with you and Mama. This brief time waiting for the OB to arrive can feel like an eternity, but they will soon enter the room and immediately either give you an "all clear, looks good" sentence or sit down to talk to you in more detail about what they want to examine more closely. The point here is that you may be sitting with your anxiety and excitement bouncing around together all throughout the appointment up and until you see the Midwife or OB at the very end. Be prepared for this, and practice your affirming "Mom Comms" along the way to try to take some of the tension out of the air.

I can tell you that the vast majority of 20-week appointments are all good news. But since this is a **Scary Moment** bit, I also must mention that your role in the event of other news is to really focus on staying connected to Mama and doing what you can to be helpful and supportive to her. No matter how bad you may feel about concerning news, understand that Mama probably feels 100x worse and is most likely blaming herself to some degree about not doing enough early on to help Baby have the best chances possible. Listen, hug, and hold. That's all you can do for now. You can talk about alternate planning and contingencies and "what if" later. Listen, hug, and hold for now. Ok, that's it for this **Scary Moment** topic, let's take a deep breath, clear our minds, and get back to the bigger picture.

Assuming everything goes well with the 20-week ultrasound appointment, getting the "all clear" here is a huge positive moment that often immediately dissolves another big chunk of everybody's anxiety. Whew! Many couples are surprised to see how much better they feel leaving this appointment with so much unconscious and unprocessed anxiety getting swept away from the pregnancy. This appointment is also when most couples find out the sex of Baby, which answers the main big question that has been on pretty much everybody's mind and has been a big topic of conversation. This knowledge also obviously can lead to finalizing Baby's name if you've gotten a head start on that process, which brings me to a little rant here.

At the end of the day, the sex of the baby and the name you choose for them are really nobody else's business, so it's perfectly understandable for you to decide not to freely share that information with any and all who ask. However, the name and sex are generally considered two easy "go to" topics for all the people around you, especially peripheral friends and family who want to show Mama that they are interested and care about how things are going. Please keep in mind that most questioning is just an attempt at what seems to be safe and polite conversation. After all, why would anybody have any legitimate reason to care whether you are having a boy or girl or what name you've chosen? People may have funny follow up questions, or not like Baby's name, but so what? It's not their baby! As long as they don't cross the line and constantly badger you about it then what does it really matter what Aunt Ethel, or anybody else, thinks about it all?

As for names, with the obvious caveat that your chosen baby name is none of my business either, just try to keep the following in mind. Don't name your baby something that they are going to have to literally spell out, letter by letter, to everybody they meet for the rest of their lives, and if you pick a common-ish name (which is totally awesome, btw), just spell it the common-ish way. "Jinyfr" is going to make your daughter hate you later on in life way more than "Jennifer" ever possibly could. Your baby's name is something that all 3 of you are going to have to live with the for the rest of your lives, so take your time choosing one that you really hope the baby will admire you for picking later on down the road. I personally like going with family names, or cool historical figures that may inspire the future young adult to look up to. But don't get too carried away. Augustus Maximus the Great might be a stretch, and things didn't end too well for other people named Genghis Khan and Julius Caesar.

Unless your family has deep roots in certain traditions and/or the family tree, nobody *really* has a vested interest in Baby being either a boy or a girl. This isn't a few years back in some places where there was huge cultural pressure to have a boy due to the fact that you only get one kid per family and girls required expensive dowries to marry off. Keep this in mind when people ask "boy or girl?" They often aren't sure what else is safe to ask about. And if you choose not to find out the sex of the baby, that's fine too. Just understand and prepare for an endless litany of "why not?" questions from anybody and everybody who asks. If you go this route it might be easier to just say "boy" whenever random people ask. A good plan B here is to give those questions absurd answers, like "chihuahua" or "pineapple" as a segue into "we'll find out soon enough." That often disrupts the question asker enough that they don't bother with the "why not?" follow up. Have fun with all of this stuff!

I know these days some folks really go all out with "gender reveal" parties, but please don't feel like you need to take it too far with this current fad. I've seen so many videos of hapless Dads timidly swinging at a pinata to see what color confetti comes out, or some other similar situation. Why so much excitement over whether Baby is a boy or girl? When asked why they did it, most of the Dads I've spoken with have all said something to the effect of "I don't know, it seemed like a really big deal to her." So, sure, go along with her on this one, just remember to do the best you can to act at least a little enthusiastic about it all so you don't get sucked into a Dud Zone here. And being pregnant has enough built in drama, no need to add more stress and manufacture extra pressure by being the one pushing Mama to do a "cool Insta-ready" gender reveal at some point. I heard of one couple who actually hired a small plane to fly over their party and spell out "It's a boy" in blue smoke. Talk about WTF? And again, this is just one thing to consider among many here in ***WTF***, take it or leave it as you see fit. ☺ Speaking of finding out Baby's sex, here's another Dad tip for you.

Dad Tip #4: From this point forward, always refer to Baby as *he/she/they* and never *"it"*. Always. 100% of the time. And once you finally decide on a name, then refer to Baby by his/her name from *that* point on. As a funny note, when my wife and I went through our first pregnancy we referred to the growing baby in her belly as "Poppy" because the very first "What to Expect When You're Expecting" video we watched super early in the pregnancy told us that Baby was the size of a poppy seed at that point. So, we went with "Poppy" all the way till week 20, and were even considering sticking with it for real if we were going to have a girl. Once we found out that we were having a boy we would refer to him by the various names we were considering up until we made our final pick, and then just stuck with that. At the end of the day, try to find a nickname or pet name to use for the growing baby instead of absent-mindedly going with "it." Remember **B1 (Instant Mama)** here, she's been in relationship with Baby since day 1 and is *definitely* not a Mama to just an "it."

Ok, back to the "just you and Mama" stuff. As I mentioned earlier, the general plan for the 2nd Trimester is for you both to take advantage of her rebound in energy to start setting the table for Baby's upcoming arrival. She is still going to be focused on taking care of herself and Baby by eating right, taking all the various vitamins and supplements, and shopping for maternity clothes that fit right. Your job is to not worry about the fact that Baby won't be here for another handful of months and to instead continue increasing your efforts to get *better connected* to Mama and *better prepared* for Baby by checking some basic things off of the to-do list. Some common things that couples figure out/buy/build during the 2nd Trimester are the following:

- car seat options (and how they integrate with the stroller options)
- stroller options
- nursery themes and décor
- baby registry items and cribs
- baby wearing devices and diaper bags

- and many other things about which that you as the Dad-to-be probably don't have too many strong opinions about at this point.

However, in order to accomplish our goals of being *better connected* to our pregnant partner and *better prepared* for Baby, you need to work as a team and find ways to tap into your preferences for giraffe or elephant stickers, black or grey car seat inserts, and small or large wheeled strollers. This whole process feels like a long, slow mental slog through thick mud for many Dads, so make sure you don't get stuck in the Dud Zones here. And remember, the sooner you get these things taken care of, the sooner you can be done thinking about them (and hearing about them...). Speaking of working as a team:

Big Idea #8: Understand the crucial difference between "teaming up" and "teaming out." Pause for a minute and consider – how often have you seen a men's synchronized swimming competition? How about all male dance teams? Never? Why do you think that is the case? In our current culture many women's basic understanding of teamwork is something like "let's do this thing over here *together*, you know, like a *team*!" And this is obviously a perfectly true and reasonable understanding of teamwork, which we'll refer to from now on as "team up." However, many men's basic understanding of teamwork is more like "I'll do this over here and you do that over there, you know, divide and conquer, like a *team*!" For our purposes here we'll call his definition "team out" to separate it from her definition of "team up". These significant differences of what it means to "work as a team" are all well and good as long as each of you is clearly communicating what your specific needs, wants, and expectations are in any given situation.

However, Mama is probably already going to be feeling all kinds of ways about "being alone" in her pregnancy as regards your role in it, and is most likely going to be looking for opportunities to create a genuine felt sense of "teamwork" with you by asking you to "team up" and do things *with* her. This dynamic is the main one at work here, and she is actually asking "*Will you team up with me in planning for our baby*?" so listen carefully for that element underneath the specific tasks that she is mentioning. That question should be pretty easy to hear when you listen to her requests with an ear for it, and therefore pretty easy to say "yes, great idea!" to it, regardless of the surface content. Dad Zone, straight ahead!

Most of these "teamwork opportunities" to *better connect* with Mama are going to involve discussing and/or shopping options for all things baby-related, such as the aforementioned car seats, strollers, cribs, room themes, etc.... Getting some *better prepared* Dad Card credits will be super easy if you are thinking along these lines of "teaming up". Misunderstanding the differences between "teaming up" vs "teaming out" can be a big and ongoing source of conflict for couples in these areas so I'll spend a few pages going over some typical scenarios and give you some extra tips on navigating them successfully and avoiding the Dud Zones. Remember, the patterns of teamwork that you are establishing and strengthening now are going to be very important foundations for your upcoming parenting adventures, so its 100% worth it to spend a little extra time and attention now on building good ones!

The challenges, or Dud Zone traps as I like to call them, in these "team up" scenarios may be extensive. Navigating them well is an important part of your future success, however, so I'll go over a few of them individually and in some detail to help you see what's in front of you here. A key dynamic to look for and understand ties back to addressing **B5 (Anxiety)** and its "push" to DO SOMETHING. In fact, "teaming up" and doing pretty much anything that releases that "push" energy is good, while not doing something will cause it to build up and eventually explode. At you. Plus, "teaming up" to go do things is a huge part of *better connecting* to Mama here, and assuming you do something somewhat constructive, it is a *better prepared* hit too. Win-win, *$ka-ching$*

Challenge 1: Many men find it hard to seriously focus on such things as car seats and strollers when the baby won't be here for several more months. For example, it's December here in Colorado as I write this and I guarantee you the percentage of men that are actively shopping for lawn mowers, patio furniture, or anything else that they won't be using until May or June is pretty close to zero. Now imagine how these men's wives and partners would respond if the men all of a sudden started really pressing their wives and partners on the *urgency* of getting those lawn mowers and patio furniture sets purchased *really soon* "so we get that taken care of!" Those women would probably look at their men like they had sprouted an extra head out of their shoulders! "Honey, WHAT are you talking about? There is a foot of snow on the ground and the grass is all dead and won't even begin to start growing for at least 4 months! WHY are we talking about lawnmowers right now?!" Seems pretty silly when we reframe this conversation, right? Nevertheless, and as mentioned a moment ago, that **B5 (Anxiety)** energy is pushing her to JUST DO SOMETHING. Getting things like the car seat, stroller, and nursery themes figured out SOON is going to be a very real thing for her. And she *absolutely* needs you to "team up" with her on these things. And now, not later.

Challenge #2: Many men aren't going to have very strong preferences about all these things. At all. I can't tell you how many dudes have basically and sincerely said "Honey, I really couldn't give a hoot about the color of the car seat insert or the whether the nursery theme is giraffes or elephants, you pick." That's reasonable, it is indeed hard to pretend that you care about something when you don't. It's also fair to be concerned about overly influencing a decision about such things when you think that the other person is much more invested in it than you are. However, this is part of your journey to the Dad Zone.

Your new understanding of how to *better connect* with Mama and be a good "teammate" here means that you will both be better served by you reorienting to wanting her to feel *helped and supported* during her pregnancy and these choices. That means putting some effort into at least having helpful discussions about the above choices and decisions, or at least staying out of the Dud Zones of Wimpytown and Jerkville with your responses. I'll help you out on this one – tell her you like the grey car seat liner better (hides milk stains easier), you like the bigger wheeled strollers (easier to go over curbs), you like the cribs with the adjustable front bars (no need to constantly bend way over a stationary crib bar for the first few months when the baby can't even roll over, much less plot an escape), and you prefer elephants to giraffes because you can make funny elephant impressions but you have no idea what a giraffe sounds like. ☺

Challenge #3: You really have NO FUCKING IDEA what to put on the baby registry or really anything else about what the baby might need, and also don't really have the interest or bandwidth to even begin to go down that particular rabbit hole. That's perfectly fine and extremely common for Dads-to-be. But again, you don't need to actually do all that much here to earn some easy Dad Card credits in these areas. First, keep in mind that you *aren't* actually responsible for figuring out and making all the "right" choices on these things. You *are*, however, 100% responsible for being present for those conversations and trips to the Baby Store and attempting to be *helpful and supportive* when discussing some of the options and ideas that come up. This is all about staying out of the Dud Zones of Wimpytown and Jerkville and helping Mama feel *better connected* to you during this journey, and much less about making the absolute best decision for Baby's registry items.

These 3 challenges can be summed up in a simple sentence most men have uttered at least one time by this point of the pregnancy journey – "I really don't know anything about these things, I also really don't have any strong preferences about them, and why are we even talking about them right now, Baby won't even be here for another 5 months!" All true, but not in line with getting to the Dad Zone and the *helpful and supportive* lens through which she is judging you, nor in line with our mantra here of *better connected* to Mama and *better prepared* for Baby.

Alright, given the above is our common starting point, let's go through a hypothetical example of how this idea of "teaming up" vs "teaming out" might play out. We'll pull out a dude from one of my workshops, Bob, and his wife Agnes. They just found out at the 20-week ultrasound that they are going to have a little girl. Agnes is now all set and ready to go on the nursery project, but doesn't want to go the all-pink route that her friend Michelle did with her baby girl last year. Agnes also doesn't want go with blue and then deal with all the stupid questions about why she picked blue for boy when she is having a girl. Therefore, this weekend she wants to head over to Lowes and look at paint options in shades of green, yellow, and purple. She is also now ready to complete the baby registry process at BuyBuyBaby, and also wants to check out some baby-wearing devices that her friends have recommended. Agnes obviously wants to hear Bob's thoughts and feelings on all of the above so she suggests they "team up" and go check these things out this coming Saturday afternoon right after their usual brunch out with friends.

Bob's first thoughts were "What? Spend all afternoon looking a paint chips and teething rings and miniature socks that barely fit on my thumb? Ugh, I'd rather go get a root canal or rectal exam." Some guys might then just sort of fall into Wimpytown and slump their shoulders in defeat and, in the interest of being *helpful and supportive*, say something like "uh, sure babe, whatever you want" as they reluctantly watch their plans slip away. Other guys might go the other way to Jerkville and then get defensive and/or miss the bigger picture and say something like "uh, no way, I don't really care about those things so why don't you go by yourself and pick whatever you want." Dud Zone alert! Neither of those responses are doing much to build up any Dad Card credits!

But not Bob, he'd been learning about "teaming up vs teaming out" and was ready to step up. Let's remember the 3 challenges I detailed above – why are we worrying about these things now; I really don't care if the nursery is yellow or green; and I don't really know anything about teething rings and 5 different kinds of bottle warmers... It was important for Bob's own sanity to allow himself a few seconds to have these thoughts and just recognize them as true-for-him. But then he quickly pushed those reactionary thoughts aside and looked at the bigger picture of his aspirations for the Dad Zone. What's the real goal here? Bob quickly pivots back to his bigger plan of getting *better connected* and realizes that what Agnes might be really asking him is just to "team up" with her and get involved in these decisions as her "teammate" in this pregnancy. But wait, Bob won't then just agree to go with her right away! Here's his chance to continue to practice his **B6 (Mom Comms).** He needs to think about how he can look at this situation to *better connect* with Mama, get some Dad Card credits, and to earn himself a few in the Man Card department here too. Here are some possible responses for him to consider, each looking to get a different kind of win-win for everybody out of this situation.

Response 1: "Sure babe, sounds great, it will be nice to get started on those things now that we know our little baby is a girl! But let's swing back home from brunch first so I can work on my garage project for a bit and so you can rest or grab a nap. We can then maybe head out around 3 or so and then hit up Outback Steakhouse (or wherever) for dinner afterwards." Win-win, *$ka-ching$.*

Response 2: "Sure babe, sounds great, it will be nice to get started on those things now that we know our little baby is a girl! And good idea for going Saturday right after brunch, I'm really looking forward to watching the game on Sunday afternoon so it's better that we go on Saturday instead and get things going." Win-win, *$ka-ching$*.

Response 3: "Sure babe, sounds great, it will be nice to get started on those things now that we know our little baby is a girl! But let's go Sunday instead? I'm planning on golfing Saturday afternoon with the guys and don't want to rush through anything. And if we go Sunday then we can make a point to hit up that new Ramen noodle joint for dinner that you mentioned last week too!" Win-win, *$ka-ching$*.

Now let's break down those responses for a minute to see what's happening there. All 3 start with the same sentence that accomplishes several things. First, Bob is immediately affirming Agnes' request to *do something now* to prepare for the baby. This addresses and calms whatever her underlying concerns might be about *not doing* something. Second, and more importantly, Bob is showing her that he is fully committed to being *better connected* to her and ready to "team up" for action. Both parts can immediately diffuse any underlying **B5 (Anxiety)** that might be driving this request and directly support our goal of getting *better connected* to Mama. And again, he is giving an enthusiastic "Yes!" to Agnes' real question underneath the specifics, which is "will you 'team up' with me in planning for the baby?" This is a critical point to get very clear on as it will play out time and time again over the next year. It's a good idea to start to train yourself to look for that theme of "teaming up" underneath the surface of the specifics of Mama's various requests and suggestions. The better you get at catching that underlying theme, the better you'll get at saying "yes" to *that* question and get Dad Card credits while also being able to work the specifics of her request into your preexisting Man Card plans that create wins for both of you. Win-win, *$ka-ching$!*

Bob's possible responses then vary considerably in what follows his "yes, and..." but the theme shown in each is that he is now working Agnes' requested trip to Lowes and BuyBuyBaby into his own weekend plans in a way where he isn't necessarily losing out on something that is important to him as the "cost" of being a "good teammate." He gets to keep his preexisting plans intact (and earn Man Card credits) and can then parlay that trip out to include a stop at a tasty restaurant that he has been thinking about recently too. This is more credit he's building in his Dad Card account, just like when you skillfully use your partner's favorite Love Languages, credit that you can cash in later for all the things that you want to do that counts as "you time," be it hitting up the bar with your buddies or knocking back a few beers on the couch watching the game. Bolster your Man Card and Dad Card credits at the same time. Bob ended up going with option 1 and got some free time in the garage and a steak dinner with a bloomin' onion out of the deal. Be like Bob! Win-win, *$ka-ching$.*

Dad Tip #5: You get double the Dad Card credits for being the one to make suggestions on *anything* related to getting ready for the baby! This requires advanced-level strategic thinking on your part though, you have to be looking at all the obvious variables and plan accordingly ahead of time. You also have to figure out the more hidden and non-obvious ones too so that you are still getting your other "wins" out of the situation beyond just the Dad Card credits. Imagine you are now in Bob's situation from above. Let's see how this **D5 (Double Credits)** might play out with the same scenario.

Scene: Wednesday evening during or after dinner.
You begin with a great lead-in... "Hey babe, I was thinking about making some more progress this weekend on getting things ready for Baby Girl. What do you think about looking at some more color options for her nursery at Lowes and then also hitting up BuyBuyBaby to fill in some gaps in her baby registry?" She immediately looks over

at you with love and pride as she sees you stepping further into the Dad Zone. Double credits! *$ka-ching$, $ka-ching$*

Then you make specific suggestions for timing while also mentioning your limits on those:

Option 1: "...Let's stick with our regular Saturday brunch plan, but then come back to the house for a bit. I want to work on that garage project after brunch and maybe you can get a nap in too. We can then head out to Lowes later in the afternoon and finish things off with dinner at Outback Steakhouse?"

Option 2: "... I'm planning on chilling on the couch Sunday afternoon to watch the game, so what do you think about heading over to Lowes right after brunch on Saturday?"

Option 3: "... I've got a tee time with the guys on Saturday afternoon and don't want to have rush things so what do you think about going out adventuring sometime on Sunday? We can also try to hit up that new Ramen joint you mentioned last week too!"

You get a lot of leeway here in the suggestion making department, so don't be too worried about "getting it right" or trying to anticipate what she may be thinking about. And remember, Mamas are quite happy and capable of working with you here too, after all, everybody prefers to find a win-win solution. You may also have noticed that in my scenarios above we're giving Mama lots of choices while also showing our commitment to being a *helpful and supportive* "teammate." This subtle use of offering options and choices is crucial for communicating where you stand. Where you end up eating dinner may not make the slightest difference to you, but giving her options and the power of choice means everything to her. Everybody likes taking turns picking dinner spots, right? At the end of the day this arena is definitely one where it is truly "the thought that counts," and making almost any suggestion to do *anything* that relates to getting *better prepared* for Baby will absolutely help you get further into the Dad Zone and accomplish the goal of getting *better connected* to Mama.

Quick recap of salient points here:

- When she makes a suggestion/request, immediately look for signs of "teaming up" being the underlying request.
- Try to say "yes" right away, and then add a validating comment into the mix when possible. "I'm glad you mentioned it, I was thinking about that the other day" is a great generic fill-in follow up for almost anything. Another angle worth considering is to compliment her amazing Mom skills here, "I'm glad you mentioned it, you are crushing this whole Mama thing already!"
- Make sure to specifically mention any time slots that you are looking to preserve. You can't read her mind, and she can't read yours. For example, don't just say "how about Sunday?" if you already had plans in the works for Saturday. Instead say "I'm planning on doing X on Saturday afternoon, how about Sunday?"
- When you want to go for double Dad Card credits and make the suggestion, you need to plan ahead or she'll beat you to it. Wednesday is probably the best day to initiate a weekend plan, but Tuesday is good too. Waiting till Thursday is pushing it...
- Mention specific options and choices in your requests, but most importantly, put firm limits around your other pre-existing plans.

Wrapping up, just imagine that 90% of what you and Mama are doing between now and when Baby gets here firmly fits into the "team up" department and NOT into your "team out" normal guy way of thinking. That will shift somewhat once Baby arrives and then the conversations will naturally turn more into what you are familiar with when thinking about "team work." You can "team out" by getting dinner going while she changes a diaper, or vice versa. There will be millions of opportunities to "team out" on parenting duties, but for now keep Mama's definition of "team up" in the front of your mind when thinking about "team work."

Remember, your goals in these conversations are to stay out of the Dud Zones of Wimpytown and Jerkville, and to make progress further into the Dad Zone by 1) helping Mama feel *better connected* to you by being a great teammate, 2) actually getting *better prepared* by accomplishing some of the things on her list (or else deal with her increased anxiety and pressure that comes from not accomplishing them), and 3) protecting your time, pre-existing obligations, and Man Card from getting swallowed up completely in Baby Land (much more on this later).

We've now covered some of the specifics of the 2nd Trimester for getting *better prepared* for Baby's arrival and how to get *better connected* to Mama in the process. Car seats, strollers, and nursery décor are the three main things that most couples try to get figured out during this 2nd Trimester. For most couples, that's about as far as they can see right now. Some couples start to make other serious life changes around this time, such as vehicle upgrades/downgrades (that 2-door Mustang just isn't going to cut it anymore), job reconsiderations (health benefits just took on a whole new sense of urgency), and housing options (your hip downtown loft might not be the most suitable for noise management and sleeping babies). We'll get into more of the specific baby-related recommendations later on, but you and your partner should definitely be having some preliminary conversations about the first 3 things above by now. And as a quick note, *absolutely nothing* is easier to deal with "once Baby arrives." Nothing. So, now is the time to get cracking!

Clicking out to the bigger picture, this next Dad Tip is a *better connected* and *better prepared* combination homerun hit deep into the Dad Zone.

Dad Tip #6: Sign up for a Birth Class. "Birth Class? What? I'm not having a baby, why do I need a 'Birth Class'? And people have been having babies for millions of years, what could you possibly learn in a Birth Class?"

Good questions, all of them, but all missing the bigger picture. Remembering the goals of getting *better connected* to Mama and *better prepared* for Baby and what lies ahead, signing up for a couples' Birth Class is one of the smartest moves you can make and is guaranteed to earn big points in the Dad Card credit department. Just think how much *better connected* she'll feel with you by her side in those classes, and how proud she'll be in telling her friends and family about your active involvement in the pregnancy, and how you're locking in Quality Time Love Language credits. Additionally, you'll definitely be getting *better prepared* and will learn plenty of things you never knew about childbirth and your very important role in the process. Win-win, *$ka-ching$!*

And heads up, there are many types of Birth Classes on offer out there. Some are a single 2-hour "workshop" type, but most are once-a-week meetings spread out over anywhere from 4 to 12 weeks. The themes and styles can vary considerably, from baby "boot camp" types to those that emphasize more natural and holistic approaches to childbirth. Like most things in the "Birth Space," Mama should have the biggest vote here on what kind of class to attend. However, you should definitely bring up the idea if she hasn't yet, and you should absolutely go to whichever one she likes best with an open mind and positive attitude. *$ka-ching$!*

One more consideration around choosing a Birth Class, it's important to remember that your fellow classmates are very likely going to be one of your main sources of "couples that are pregnant too and will be having a baby around the same time as us so we'll probably end up hanging a lot with the ones we like the most." More importantly, it gives Mama a big boost in her number of "other Mamas that know exactly what I'm going through right now." You want her to have as many of these other pregnant friends as possible, for both your sakes! For that reason, it's important to consider the philosophical ideology of the type of Birth Classes that you are considering. For example, my wife and I are a bit "Progressive New Age Hippie-ish" (obviously, or I wouldn't be writing this book, right?) so we signed up for a Birth Class that emphasized natural pain management techniques and was designed to help the couples have what they call a "low-intervention" birth. We ended up meeting a bunch of other like-minded couples and became good friends with several of them and hung out with them outside of the classes both before and after our babies came into the world. This friend finding task is a lot easier to manage if you are thinking about these things ahead of time when choosing a Birth Class.

Our last timely topic to cover here in the 2nd Trimester could perhaps be the most important move you can make throughout the whole pregnancy, so listen carefully here...

Dad Tip #7: Dude, hire a Doula! If you are like most guys and are new to the whole "Birth Space" field and all its unique phrasing, language, and terminology, then you most likely have no idea what a Doula is or does. So, a Doula is essentially a "birth professional" who you hire to personally accompany and assist you and your pregnant partner through the process of childbirth. They will be your trusted guide and helper each step of the way through the rest of the pregnancy also. Your Doula will most likely be a woman who has been through, assisted with, and/or witnessed anywhere from 10 – 100's of other babies being born, and who feels very connected to idea of being a positive "helper" for both of you. She is explicitly there to help Mama (and you) through all of the non-medical components of childbirth. The fee for the service can vary widely depending on how extensive the Doula's involvement will be throughout the remainder of the pregnancy and birth, and these days many doulas offer virtual services for more affordable rates. Regardless of whether the Doula supports you in person or virtually, this fee includes everything from helping your partner remain as comfortable as possible throughout labor & delivery, coaching you up on different ways to be *helpful and supportive*, and about 100 other things. However, the two most important things a Doula provides cannot be necessarily measured or quantified and are as follows:

1) Your Doula becomes your pregnant partner's trusted and go-to source for all things related to her pregnancy. She's like an awesome big sister/best friend/counselor combo all wrapped up in one package. She's a one-stop shop for the entire community of support we don't have any more to help pregnant Mamas as described in **B2 (Different World)**. Mama gets a dedicated partner that she feels like she can count on 100% throughout the rest of the pregnancy and the birth process, which is an amazing and invaluable thing. While a significant expense for sure, this is seriously the best possible use of that kind of money *anywhere* throughout the whole pregnancy journey.
2) Your Doula also becomes a "wingman from Heaven" for you, especially once shit gets real and Mama starts going into serious labor and can't help but freak out a little bit and is looking to you to hold her whole world together as you are freaking out too. You will be SOOOOOO much better off through labor and Baby being born if you have a Doula by your side helping both you and Mama through what will likely be the most intense 24 hours of both of

your lives up until this point. TRUST ME ON THIS! Seriously, if you do nothing else that I recommend in this book other than hire a Doula then you will have gotten tremendous value from it.

Ok, so how do you go about hiring a Doula? I recommend that you interview at least 3 different candidates for the job and then ultimately go with whichever one Mama feels best about. Just like in any interview process, make sure you ask each of the candidates the same questions in the same order to help you compare apples to apples. And obviously you want to find a Doula who's "birth philosophy" lines up very closely with yours too. Here are some good questions to include in your interview list:

- What do understand your main job to be in your role as Doula?
- What are your preferred natural pain management techniques?
- What support do you provide your couples prior to going into labor?
- What specific services do you provide once labor begins?
- Please share with us some of your favorite Birth Stories? (More on Birth Stories later...)
- Please share some stories of more challenging births you've witnessed, and how you were able to make a positive difference?
- What do you think is the best way for the Dad to support his partner through labor and delivery?
- Have you previously worked with our OB, Midwife, and/or chosen birth destination?

In addition to being your loyal wingman and advocate through the actual childbirth, most Doulas will also plan to meet up or chat on the phone with both you and Mama about once a month-ish up until the around the 36th week, at which point the check-ins will probably increase to about once a week or so. They will help you get your Birth Plan figured out, your Go-Bag put together, and a few other things such as who you want in the room with you, your birth meal requests, and your plan for going back home. (Don't worry guys, we'll cover all these things in later chapters. ☺)

All right, that pretty much wraps up this 2nd Trimester part of the journey. This middle ground is a relatively easy stretch of time, allowing both you and Mama to get used to idea of becoming parents and for starting to build some momentum and make progress in preparing your lives and home for the upcoming arrival of Baby. You'll need this momentum as you head into the 3rd Trimester and continue to focus on Baby's entry into the world. That day will be here sooner than you think!

Chapter 3 Summary for You: As you enter into the 2nd Trimester you should be pretty firmly anchored in the **B7 (Birth Space)** and are now ready to increase your efforts in getting *better connected* to Mama and *better prepared* for Baby's arrival. After 12 weeks many couples have the official pregnancy announcement as their first big "going public" moment. The second big public moment follows the 20-week ultrasound appointment when you should be able to determine Baby's sex. This appointment can be **Scary Moment #2** and is often the biggest deal of the entire 2nd Trimester for many couples. From that point forward keep **D4 (Not an "It")** in mind and always use "he," "she," or "they" when referring to Baby, and never "it." Even better is using this new knowledge as a way to help finalize a name choice by playing with the various names being considered to see how they fit and feel. Last point on this topic, telling people the sex/name of the baby and/or having a big "gender reveal" party are your personal choices, but try not to get too worked up about them or offended when asked those questions pretty much constantly by everybody.

Here in the 2nd Trimester you will also have many increasing opportunities to continue to practice your "Mom Comms" and Love Language skills developed earlier in **B6 (Mom Comms),** and will have opportunities to earn lots of Dad Card and Man Card credits through **B8 (Teamwork)** and "teaming up" as Mama understands the term, and to earn your **D5 (Double Credits)** for being the one to initiate plans. These opportunities are all good stepping up into the Dad Zone moments, but beware the allure of hanging out too long in the Dud Zones of Wimpytown and Jerkville if you notice yourself drifting that way. This is now the time to ramp up your planning for Baby and to bolster your "Birth Space" knowledge and abilities by signing up for a **D6 (Birth Class)** and also looking into hiring a **D7 (Doula)**.

Chapter 3 Summary for Mama: We brought Dad up to speed on how this 2nd Trimester is often considered the sweet spot of the pregnancy where your energy levels are picking back up and you are feeling a little better about many things. We suggested that this is the time for relaxing into your pregnancy and making the most out of this sunset period of your relationship with Dad as "just a couple". So, enjoy this golden time together as a party of two, but also put some effort into *better connecting* with Dad where he is on his journey by encouraging him to continue to enjoy his own interests and hobbies now while he still has time and energy to do so. We talked to Dad about this, and also suggested you seek out a new hobby you both enjoy and can run with from now on. If you have waited until now for the official "Pregnancy Announcement," then have some fun getting Dad involved a little bit in how you want to go about things, but feel free to take the lead here.

As far as getting *better prepared* for Baby, we told Dad that now is the time to start to make a big push for getting the baby basics all set up, and this includes the registry, nursery set up, car seat and stroller, and other such things. Keep in mind that Dad may be pretty oblivious to these things as a whole, has likely spent zero time thinking about them ever in his whole life before now, and will be more than slightly confused as to why getting them now is such a priority when Baby's arrival is still months away. Please be patient with his slower process and lack of urgency here, and remember that you'll get more interest and effort from him on these topics and choices by keeping your questions to *narrow specifics*, like "which of these 2 baby monitors do you like better?" rather than "wow, look at these 20 baby monitor options, what do you think?"

The same goes for almost all of the baby registry items. He probably has no opinion on teething rings, or onesies, or most such things. And that's OK. He does, however, have a very high interest in you being happy and excited about them, so feel free to take the lead on all these things and just ask him to chip in an opinion here and there.

Please remember that his idea of "team" is probably much more of a "team out," divide-and-conquer approach than your notion of "teaming up" to work on things together. We explained this difference to him and stressed the importance of "teaming up" with you in planning and preparing for Baby. On occasion, play to his definition of "team out," like the next time you go to Target or somewhere together. Ask him to go bang out the grocery list while you do a leisurely stroll through the baby section on your own rather than you both sticking together the whole time. Throw in some random high-fives and "good teamwork babe" to help him feel appreciated too.

I also strongly recommend looking into taking a couple's Birth Class together as well as hiring a Doula now that you are in the 2nd Trimester. Both of these things will help bring him deeper into the Dad Zone and the "Birth Space" and *better connected* to you and to where you are in the journey. He still won't be anywhere as deep into it as you are, but these things will help bring him further along, which will help you both feel *better connected* to each other and *better prepared* for Baby's arrival.

Finally, we talked about how your much anticipated 20-week ultrasound appointment will likely bring you good news on Baby's health and also reveal Baby's sex, allowing you both to refine your focus on the right name for Baby. This should be a fun way to "try on" the various names with each other and with your friends and family, but don't get too caught up in other people's reactions. Your friends and family will be much more impressed by your emerging Mom skills if you don't go for a high drama, gender reveal party here and instead keep things simple and easy. Mom life is already going to be hard enough, so now is a good time as any to look to get ahead of things and start to prune out any rising feelings of competitive parenting.

Chapter 4
The 3rd Trimester

Giddy up, Cowboy!!

Things are really going to accelerate here for both you and Mama as you enter the 3rd Trimester, covering roughly weeks 28 through childbirth. Remembering our roller coaster analogy, you're now nearing the crest of the hill and are probably starting to freak out a little bit about how this thing is MUCH, MUCH higher than it looked from way back on the ground 4 or 5 months ago. By this point you have (ideally) got the basics of the nursery set up (crib built and décor decided), got your car seat and stroller picked out and purchased, and are taking Birth Classes and have hired a Doula. Anything above that you haven't done, get on it.

As I mentioned earlier, your role in the pregnancy steadily increases in both activity and intensity as time goes on, so there will be a lot more to this chapter than the previous ones. No **Big Ideas** for this section, but a whole bunch of specific **Dad Tips** to help you get *better connected* to your pregnant partner during this home stretch and get *better prepared* for the impending arrival of Baby! FYI, upcoming **Dad Tips #8, 9**, and **10** are definitely "do these now", while **#11 - 15** can be delayed to closer to week 34 or so. Don't push those off much past then though, or you could find yourself unexpectedly rushing off to the birth center, wondering how you found yourself there so unexpectedly and unprepared!

Checking in with Mama's development, she is definitely fully showing her baby bump by now, and her belly will only get bigger and rounder as the weeks go on. She may develop some new aches and pains in her hips and back, experience increased urination and fatigue, have trouble sleeping, bouts of Braxton-Hicks contractions (basically minor warm-up "practice" contractions), and even more increased anxiety as the expected due date creeps closer (yay). She might also start to more aggressively question how prepared *you* seem to be for Baby's upcoming arrival and begin to more vocally pressure you on picking up the pace in getting into the Dad Zone in areas she feels you lagging behind. Remember **B5 (Anxiety)**, her anxiety is real and needs to push on something, and you're naturally going to be the main target! All good though, and this chapter will cover plenty of things that you can do right now to help minimize that last one.

As for Baby, the 28th week marks the end of the 2nd Trimester and the beginning of the 3rd Trimester, mainly because from this point onward Baby is generally considered able to survive outside the womb on their own (but obviously needing the help of modern medicine and advanced NICU [Neonatal Intensive Care Unit] support if they come out on the early side of this window). Most of Baby's growth from 28 weeks to birth is in packing on the pounds and continuing brain and neuron development. Baby starts this 3rd Trimester around 15 inches and 2 pounds but will finish up somewhere between 19 – 21 inches long and weighing somewhere between 6 – 10 pounds. Babies that come before 37 weeks are considered premature (preemie), and are considered "full term" from week 37 onward. However, most babies don't show up until somewhere around the 40-week mark, and some even wait till closer to 42 weeks to join us here on the outside! This 5 to 6-week window of variability around the "due date" is a very, very different lived reality for Mama than not having a package showing up on your front porch on its "delivery date," which leads us right into our next Dad Tip.

Dad Tip #8: STOP talking about "Due Date" and START talking about "Expected Arrival." There are few things that seem to cause more anxiety in our pregnant partners than the idea of a concrete "due date." I've seen more than a few pregnant women look at this "due date" as if it were a guaranteed set thing marked on their calendars with a Sharpie, like having another OB appointment or going on a planned vacation. The fact is that only about 5% of all babies actually arrive on their due date! As mentioned earlier, "Full term" is used to describe all babies that arrive from the 37th week up till 42 weeks – that's over a month of variability! Now is a good time to remember our **B6 (Mom Comms)** philosophy on the importance of subtle distinctions in language and phrasing. If you haven't already done so, start shifting your language and begin using vaguer phrases like "the end of March" instead of a single date like "March 24th" when you are discussing Baby's expected arrival. You'll have plenty of time to practice this with friends, family, and strangers alike when they all ask "When is the baby coming?"

You'll definitely need to redirect this "due date" conversation when you're only having it at home with Mama as the time gets closer too. Whatever you can say to shift her attention off that specific date will (sort of) help her anxiety around the baby's arrival subside a little bit. I recommend continuously using phrases like "when the baby is ready," "in the next few weeks or so," and "soon enough" to help shift her focus off just that specific date. You'll be more effective here if she feels that your redirection is coming from a place of *connection* and *preparedness* rather than from a lack of concern with Baby's timing, so try to pair your efforts with a few reminders about how ready you both are for when Baby does decide to show up. However, in spite of your best efforts, Mama may seem largely immune your suggestions to move her attention away from that specific date. Remembering **B4 (Biggest Deal)** and **B5 (Anxiety)**, the "due date" is when all this finally goes down and she gets to meet her baby! How could she *not* be focused on this date with ALL her emotions turned up to 10? But plod on in your efforts, they are a good counterpoint for her to lean into and will be helpful for her to hear calmly and consistently as "the due date" approaches. Even if she says nothing, your calming assurances and reframing of this idea ARE getting through, trust me on this.

Here's a good personal anecdote around this particular **Dad Tip** for you to consider. Our first baby had a "due date" of July 30th, and from about July 20th onward my lovely and amazing wife was 100% stressed and obsessed with Baby's arrival. It was mid-summer in Omaha, so she was huge, hot, and entirely fed up with being pregnant. Her hips and back were hurting so bad that we went to the pool every afternoon just so she could hang by her elbows off the edge of the pool and float in the water for a while to take the pressure off her hips, back, and feet. By the time the 29th rolled around she was eating 20 figs a day (supposedly they help "bring the baby"), walking around as much as possible (supposedly walking helps "bring the baby"), and doing countless other things to help "bring the baby" out into our world. One of her friends had just flown in (with round trip tickets she had purchased 3 months prior focused on the "due date") to help around the house after Baby arrived, but was then left fretting and wringing her hands in delayed anticipation as July ended and August started up. Every day brought more questions and "helpful" comments, like "I really hope the baby comes today" and "are your contractions starting yet?" Not much fun for anyone!

As a reminder, my wife is a pretty amazing woman. Confident, smart, strong, and also a Pediatric Nurse Practitioner, so she knows almost all there is to know about babies and due dates. Yet even with all her knowledge and medical training she was still practically losing her mind with anxiety and impatience about Baby "being late." And none of these feelings of anxiety were being helped by her friend's hovering anticipation.

Finally, Baby decided he was ready to come out and he joined us late afternoon on Aug 5th, thankfully the day before the "helpful friend" was scheduled to fly back home. Needless to say, those last 2 weeks before he was born were probably the hardest part of the pregnancy for my wife, mainly due to her building anticipation and then growing frustration and worry as the "due date" came and went. Fast forward two years later and we were pregnant again with our daughter, and even though the "due date" was June 13th, we both told ourselves (and everybody else) that she was due in "mid-June" to try to eliminate or minimize the pressure of the expectations of a set date. Baby Girl arrived 5 days "late" on the 18th, but into a much less frenzied and stressed household this time around that wasn't all wrapped up in how "late" she was in coming.

Dad Tip #9: Put yourself in charge of the Gift Tracker Spreadsheet. You will be receiving a ton of baby-related gifts and things around this time and going forward, many of which may be things not on your official Baby Registry. Your first reaction to all these tiny socks, onesies, teething rings, and who knows what else might be something like "uh, here you go Mama, put these things wherever you want I guess." Not wrong, but definitely not a Dad Zone type of answer and not one gets you *better connected* to Mama nor *better prepared* for when Baby comes.

A great solution that will accomplish both of the above and also get you huge Dad Card Credits is for you to be the one to create a "Gift Tracker Spreadsheet," or GTS. The GTS is just a simple document that you create that includes the following – the gift giver (Aunt Edna), date received, an accurate description of the gift (blue onesie with the train on the front), place stored, and picture sent boxes. I've included a sample template for you to see in Appendix C at the end of the book as well as in the Reference section of the ***WTF*** website. For a bit of extra insurance take a picture of each gift and create a file in your phone's camera app where you store all the incoming gift photos. Now, here is a key detail – store ALL the gifts in the *same place* for now (excepting perhaps nursery decorations or things that you are actually using now). Please remember that all the gift giver really wants in return is to see a picture of the baby wearing/using/playing with the gift that was sent. So, after Baby comes, you can then get out the GTS and starting creating opportunities to take pictures of them wearing/using/playing with the various gifts that you've been tracking. Once you have taken a picture of Baby wearing the blue onesie with the train on it and sent it to Aunt Edna you can then cross that item off of your GTS. Boom, done!

A down the road pro-tip for managing the GTS is for you and Mama to take advantage of a random weekend afternoon when Baby is in a great mood and just go through your GTS line by line and knock out as many items as you can. Just think of it as a baby fashion show as you are working your way through the pile of various things and sending out pic after pic, all captioned "Thank you, little Mikey just loves this shirt/onesie/jacket/toy!" Even for that silly Uncle who sent you the cute wooden train set clearly labeled "For ages 2 and up," get the trains out for a hot minute and take a pic of Baby lying next to them, and "boom!", one more name scratched off the list! Once you get all your pics of each of the items you can then move those items out of the stash and to wherever they will ultimately go, be it the changing table, toy bin, or donation pile. You are officially in the clear on every gift that has been taken out of the stash, photo-op-ed, and then marked off the GTS. But all of that is for much later on. Back to making the GTS in the first place, Mama will be ecstatic that you are *better connecting* with her by helping manage the gifts. You can ask her to sit down with you once a week or so and help you keep the GTS up to date as things show up on your porch also. Using the GTS wisely will help you continue your progress into the Dad Zone and also help you get *better prepared* and more familiar with all those things baby-related that are starting to pile up in the nursery closet. Win-win, *$ka-ching$*

Super Pro-tip: Baby showers can be tricky. Most Dads-to-be I've worked with had a pretty low interest in getting sucked into the one being thrown for their Baby, but a pretty high interest in getting *better connected* to Mama and her journey. Option 1 for the baby shower is to partner up with some of the significant other dudes of the attending guests and go out golfing or hiking or watching a game together. If you go this route then make sure to mention to Mama that you are planning to hit them up for some good How-to-be-a-Dad intel during this time together in order to get some easy Dad Card credits. However, Option 2 is worth considering also. In this option you attend the gift giving part of the baby shower, GTS in hand to keep track of all the various gifts and presents. As you are fervently getting pics of everything and writing down who gave what, Mama's friends will be filled with wonder and awe about how *helpful and supportive* you are being, much to Mama's pride and delight. Mama's friends seeing you being awesome? Talk about earning serious Dad Card credits! Win-win, *$KA-CHING$!*

Dad Tip #10: Top Ten Baby Registry Items (for Dads). The following list covers the top ten things, in no particular order, that I think will make your lives as new parents much easier and more enjoyable, especially for you as the Dad. You obviously won't be using them anytime soon, but better to put them on the registry or buy them yourselves now and be done with it.

1. A Tummy Tub. This is essentially a translucent bucket with a rounded interior that you use to give Baby a bath. You only need to put a few ounces of warm water in it and the rounded bottom is super cozy for Baby. Importantly, because it is translucent, you are instantly aware of any of Baby's potentially unwelcome "contributions" to the bath water. You

can use it from birth up to and over 1 year of age, and bath time can be one of the most fun daily family bonding rituals, especially as Baby gets a little bit older and starts splashing around and going crazy in the Tummy Tub.

2. White noise machines. A whole bunch to strategically place around the house. "White noise" in a shushing, rhythmic, ocean wave-like pattern mimics the sounds of Mama's womb and is very calming to a baby. The womb is a loud place, like 90 decibels, so having what sounds like waves practically crashing on top of your head can actually be very helpful and relaxing to Baby, especially one that is upset and not easily soothed. White noise is your best friend when it comes to getting, and keeping, Baby asleep. Ideally you have the option to turn on a white noise machine within 5 feet of wherever Baby is sleeping at any given time to help mask out other sounds that might wake them up. Trust me, one of the most disappointing sounds in the world is your baby crying after only being asleep for 5 minutes, unexpectedly woken up due to your neighbor's dog barking, a horn honking, or the phone ringing.
3. The Shusher. AKA, your portable white noise machine and magic wand. The Shusher is a small, hand-held and battery-powered white noise machine that has a built-in timer and is meant to be used anywhere and everywhere you and your baby might be. Imagine a long car ride (or even a short one) with a screaming baby, or trying to rock a crying baby back to sleep in the middle of the night and huffing and puffing your own "shhhhh!!!" sounds for 20 minutes straight. The Shusher is your savior!!
4. Wireless over-ear headphones with noise cancellation feature. The sound of a baby crying is one of the most psychologically destructive sounds on the planet. While it has been shown to provoke extreme anxiety in many women, it has also been shown to provoke extreme anger in many men. No joke, and

more on this later when we get to the "New Dad Blues" section, but make sure you have a pair of these in the house before the baby comes home. It is MUCH, MUCH, MUCH easier to be physically and emotionally present for your crying baby, lovingly rocking them back and forth with the Shusher at your side at 4am for the third night in a row, when you are using your headphones to block out all the sharpest edges of the crying. A good pair of them can get a little expensive, but consider it a worthy investment in your sanity. You can listen to podcasts, your favorite music, or hook it up to your TV to catch the game – all while cuddling and caring for your baby like the awesome Dad that you are!

5. A Dad diaper bag. One that is slimmed down to just carry what you need on that short afternoon stroll up to the park and back, and that you really like. Many a woman's diaper bag can quickly expand to include over a hundred other things besides 2 diapers and some wipes. Ointments, lotions, sunscreen, back-up onesies, pacifiers, Chapstick, the list goes on and on. And all good things to have for when you need them. But rather than A) dragging that whole thing with you when you take the baby to the grocery store so that Mama can actually get in a full shower and a nap for once, or B) trying to strip it down to the essentials and then carrying a giant, mostly-empty floral tote around for 2 hours, you can just grab your always ready Dad Bag and head out the door. I'd recommend a few diapers, wipes, back-up outfit in a Ziplock bag (the plastic bag is for the diaper blow-out situation that went down that requires you to use the back-up outfit in the first place…), pacifier, and Shusher. That way she gets "the" diaper bag to set up however she wants and you have yours to do the same. Fewer discussions over such things is better for all 3 of you. Final tip on the Dad Bag – get one with a hard and flat bottom. Nothing is more annoying than trying to avoid getting baby

shit everywhere while you constantly struggle with a diaper bag that keeps falling over on its side and closing on you.

6. *All* the Frida Baby stuff. Seriously, this company has these things figured out. Snotsucker? Yes! What, you think your baby knows how to blow its own nose? And Frida Fever is fantastic. It's essentially a stick-on, band-aid type device with a sensor that you access through an app on your smartphone that constantly tracks your baby's temperature during a bout of illness. Back in the day my Mom had to take our temperatures *rectally* every hour to track a fever. Sounds fun for both you and the baby, eh? The Frida Fever is one of many awesome products this company makes, get them all. I don't get any kick-backs for mentioning this company or any other, but you emailing me later and profusely thanking me for telling you about them is pretty nice.
7. Dock-a-tot. This is basically exactly what it sounds like. You dock your tot in it for short periods of time. Think of a mesh pet-bed like thing that is baby-sized and surrounded by a 4-inch foam bumper. This is great for any and all non-crib naps. For instance, imagine you have happily rocked your baby to sleep and now want to, say, make a sandwich, go to the bathroom, or any other normal activity that is rendered almost impossible to do when holding a sleeping baby. With some supervision, the Dock-a-tot can be used on the couch, the floor, the kitchen table, pretty much any firm surface. The mesh part is super soft and the foam bumpers keep the baby safe and secure. Sleeping Baby equals happy parents.
8. Baby wearing device. These things are all the rage now and come in many types, makes, and models. My wife and I opted for a "convertible" ruck sack style that we can wear on either our front or back (Baby facing either in or out too), and it has several straps that easily adjust for whatever changes we need to make to the fit when we take turns wearing it. You can find all kinds of cool wraps, slings, and rucksacks out on the market

these days, but anything that you and your pregnant partner both like will be great. Wearing a baby when you are out and about gets you huge Dad Card credits from everybody, and its *way* easier than just carrying your baby in your arms or dealing with the hassle of a stroller all the time. And babies always prefer to snuggle up close to you or Mama when possible. Again, win-win, *$ka-ching$.*

9. Pacifier clips. These are basically just little metal clips with a short fabric run that attaches to your baby's pacifier (if you are OK with using pacifiers, of course). They come in all varieties and textures and are great sanity savors for both you and Baby. Pacifier comes out of Baby's mouth when you're driving? Easy-peasy, just feel around blindly for the clip and pop it back in Baby's mouth. No clip means you have no idea where it went in the car, leaving Baby to get madder and madder and louder and louder. You then search for the lost pacifier frantically when you arrive, only to eventually find it covered in whatever has been building up deep under your seat for the past 5 years. These clips are also cool because you can get them in every kind of print and pattern, from dinosaurs to team themes, like the Philadelphia Eagles for example. Go Birds!
10. Crockpot/Instapot. We'll go over this item in more detail later as we plan for coming back home with brand new Baby, but go ahead and get it now if you don't already have one. And if you do have one already, great, break it out and start figuring out how to set it up and what kinds of recipes you both like. Trust me on this one, one of your biggest Dad Zone moves down the road if/when you go back to work after Baby comes is to set up the crockpot in the morning for the evening's dinner as you get ready to head out the door. One of a new Mama's favorite phrases to hear is "I already have dinner set up in the crockpot, it will be ready to eat any time after 5pm."

That pretty much covers the "do these things right away" section of the chapter, let's now move a bit closer to the "expected arrival" window of Baby and focus on some **Dad Tips** that you can bring into play from weeks 34 onward.

Dad Tip #11: Take a field trip with your pregnant partner to wherever you expect to give birth to the baby. This type of recon is a *better connected, better prepared* combo home run and is critical to your number 1 objective from Labor onwards – being Attentive, Calm, and Competent (we'll go over these 3 ideas in *much* more detail in the next chapter.) The things you want to have nailed down here in your field trip are Route, Parking, and the Labor & Delivery building layout. Plan A is your most obvious and expedient route from your house to the hospital or birth center or wherever your first choice of having the baby happens to be located. Also get an alternative Plan B route set up in case you need it. On this particular field trip, take your Plan B route to your birth destination and your Plan A route home, again assuming the Plan A route is the more obvious and familiar one. Make a note of prominent landmarks and whatnot to help you navigate whatever your various turns and exits might be. Remember, there is a good chance Mama will be in the passenger seat with strong contractions going on when you are making this trip for real. You too will likely be in a highly excited and emotional state, not really the best time to be learning a new route! Mama will not be interested or available to help you figure out how to get there, and the last thing you need to hear about for the rest of your life is how you got lost going to the hospital when the baby was coming (the Birth Story, and your role in it, will be covered in the next chapter).

Once you get to the hospital or birth center make sure to thoroughly check out the various parking options. Think about this for a minute. You don't want to make your laboring partner walk from the 3rd level of some random parking garage all the way to the front door of the building, right? You also don't want to just drop her off at the curb to sit and wait by herself while you go search for a parking spot. She ABSOLUTELY will NOT be happy if you try that move! You'll then be hearing about how you just "abandoned her at the curb" when Baby was coming for the rest of your life. So, first look to see if there is a Valet option, pretty common at Labor & Delivery entrances at most hospitals these days, as that will be your go-to move when Baby is actually coming. If there is no Valet option, talk to somebody at the front desk to see if they can send somebody out to the curb with a wheel chair when you are actually coming in hot at 2am with a baby on the way. Whatever you do, DO NOT have your plan to be to just drop your laboring partner off at the curb by herself while you find a parking spot!

After you have figured out your parking plans, make a point to go visit the Labor & Delivery unit. They will happily give you a tour (easiest when arranged ahead of time) so that you can see exactly how the rooms are set up, where to get coffee and snacks, and how they manage friends and family visitors. You'll want to make a point to make sure you know exactly how to get to L&D from the front door, and also how to get to and from the hospital's café from L&D. I'd even recommend that you do this site visit *twice* just to make sure that you and your partner (and Doula) are all on the exact same page and comfort level with how everything is laid out. You might even make note of what views are out what windows in case that is relevant to you or your partner. While you probably won't be able to get your favorite corner room when you eventually show up in labor, you might at least be able to request a room along a South wall that gets more sunshine, or whatever your preferences might be, if you know those things ahead of time.

Dad Tip #12: Get your "Go Bag" 100% stocked and ready. Your "Go Bag" is simply a carry-on piece of luggage or two that has all the things you might need for your hospital stay during labor, delivery, and recovery time. This bag should have everything you, Mama, and your new little Baby will need for the approximately 48 hours or so that you will be away from home. For you this bag will look like a basic overnighter with a few changes of clothes and your usual toiletries, but for Mama (and Baby) you'll need more than that. Therefore, you'll want to "team up" with Mama and assemble this Go Bag together. This move will obviously earn you some more *better connected* Dad Card credits too. You can find many lists of suggested items to include in the Go Bag online, and Mama has probably already looked into this pretty thoroughly by now too. You can also check out Appendix D or the Reference section of the ***WTF*** website for a good starter Go-Bag checklist. If Mama already has this list covered, I'd recommend that you check it to be sure the following items are included:

- Extension cord and power strip
- Laptop and charger
- Bluetooth speaker and charger
- A refillable water bottle
- A few packs of instant coffee and some favorite snacks

Here's the deal. You may find yourself tethered to your laboring partner for many hours at a time. The extension cord and power strip will allow you to utilize an otherwise inconvenient power outlet to keep your phone, her phone, your speaker (playing soothing tunes for her), and whatever else you might need (heated blanket, power massager, etc....) all within easy reach. Your refillable water bottle keeps her and you happily hydrated, and your instant coffee and snacks give you a quick boost of energy whenever you might need it (such as at 3 am when there is no coffee readily available).

A concern I often heard from the guys in my workshops is that they use many of the Go Bag items at home on a regular basis, such as the laptop and Bluetooth speaker, so don't want to pack them all up out of use for a several weeks. Good point, fellas. What I recommend to do here is to make a list of all the items you want to bring with you that aren't going to be stashed away and simply put that list inside the Go Bag right on top of the rest of your stuff. When the time comes to head out you can then quickly check your list and retrieve the final items you need to get the Go Bag actually ready to go.

PS – If you have pets make sure that you have plans in place ahead of time for them to be taken care of for the duration of your absence, preferably a neighbor who you can contact on short notice. "Hey Jeff, sorry for texting you at 3am but we are headed to the hospital now, Jenn's labor is getting intense. As we discussed earlier, can you please let Sammy out later this morning and give him his breakfast before you go to work? Mary is coming over around noon or so to give him a walk and will do so again around 9 tonight, so please just pop back in around 5 or so when you get home from work to let him out again and feed him dinner. I'll be in touch with baby news as things develop. Thanks again!"

Dad Tip #13: The Birth Plan, and related decisions – know your choices. There are many, many, many options and choices around Baby's arrival that should be explored and considered during the 3rd Trimester. You and Mama should be discussing such things as breast feeding strategies (do you have a breast pump yet?), diaper choices (cloth vs disposable), family & friend helper visits immediately after the baby is born, child care options for when Mama's maternity leave ends, and many other baby-related plans. One of the biggest topics that you want to make sure that you are both really clear about is what's called the Birth Plan. The Birth Plan covers most of the details and decisions you need to make about the actual childbirth process and follow-up care. You can find many examples of Birth Plans online, and you've probably already had some preliminary discussions about many of the things covered therein. For your convenience I've also put a simple Birth Plan template in Appendix E at the end of the book and in the Reference section of the ***WTF*** website. Ideally your final

Birth Plan will be just one page, and put together with input from your Doula and Midwife or OB. You can then break it out to review again with your specific delivery room team upon checking in at the hospital or birth place when Baby is coming.

Topics covered in the Birth Plan include mood of the delivery room (low lights and soft music), cervical checking frequency, pain management preferences, food and beverage preferences, who's allowed in the room (med students? Family?), placenta encapsulation (yes that's a thing, and yes, I recommend it), and many other things. The Birth Plan also covers some cool opportunities for you to get more involved, like being the one to cut the umbilical cord, for example. It is very important for you and Mama to look into those things now and educate yourself about all the choices that you have regarding your delivery experience. Remember, hospitals deliver babies all day long, every day. While for you and Mama the Baby's birth is likely the biggest event of your lives together so far, for those folks it's just another ho-hum Tuesday of delivering babies. They have their systems in place to expedite the process for them while also providing maximum protection for Mama and Baby. You may or may not fit the typical profile for people having a baby, so it's your job to clearly communicate your preferences ahead of time to the staff working that day. I strongly recommend that you construct and review your Birth Plan's preferences with your OB/Midwife/Doula team to make sure that you are working within the rules and regulations of the hospital or alternative birthing destination.

Now please don't go overboard and get too worked up over every detail possible, just keep your Birth Plan to a *single page* and understand that a "successful birth" is one facilitated by all parties working together for the safety and comfort of both Mama and Baby. An example I often use with the guys is to treat this whole birth situation as if you are planning a very special date with Mama at a super fancy restaurant. Let's explore this analogy. Go there ahead of time and scope the place out. Figure out where you would like to sit. Look over the menu to make sure that you are aware of your choices and that you are certain Mama will like the place. When you make your reservation, make sure to inform them that it is a special date and you'd like to request a good table and a good waiter. You can also then tell them that you want to preorder the chocolate souffle for dessert and that you would like "Happy Anniversary" written on the plate with chocolate syrup and also have a candle on there too. Most any restaurant would happily accommodate such simple requests if made ahead of time, ensuring that you have an awesome experience to remember.

Now, compare the above scenario with just showing up randomly and getting sat wherever, with whomever as your waiter, with nobody knowing (or caring) that this is a "big night" for you. You might still have a good experience, but probably not as good as if you had put a little more effort into planning for these things. As the saying goes – "If you buy the standard hospital ticket, you get the standard hospital ride." At the end of the day your Birth Plan should be put together with the simple idea that you are trying to customize your experience in alignment with your preferences, but should also still stick well within the basic normal operations of your place of birth. Remember, a "successful" childbirth is one that ends with a healthy Baby and healthy Mama, not one that follows the Birth Plan line by line.

A final topic to focus on in the Birth Plan is for you and Mama to choose somebody to be your birth communication point of contact: a single person you keep informed of all things Labor & Delivery related, who then keeps all the other relevant folks informed. You want to have just one friend or family member picked out who is going to be in charge of notifications and updates about going into Labor, all the stuff that goes down at the hospital, and the ultimate arrival of Baby. Most people go with Mama's sister or her Mom, or even a best friend, but anybody who can be trusted to handle your business the way you want them to is just fine. This person needs to be provided a list of pre-screened VIPs that you want to keep posted on your situation, along with their respective phone numbers and/or email addresses. This point person can then be the only person who you have to call or text to tell them "we are going to the birth destination now," followed by the occasional progress update, and then followed by the "Our baby is here!" This person will then provide the various updates to all the VIP's along with strict reminders not to blow up your phones until they hear from you directly over the next couple of days because, you know, you're kind of busy having a baby.

I know this idea may seem pretty restrictive and that you are wondering why you can't just text or call any and all the people you want to let them know what's going on. And you can if you like. But please keep in mind that having your phone constantly dinging with messages and phone calls from everybody wanting to "check in" with you can be very distracting and annoying when you and Mama are in the middle of a few hours (or more) of active labor. Most annoying to Mama will be you reaching for the phone and trying to text out all kinds of updates while she is moaning and screaming at you for not helping her. You don't want "and he was on the phone the whole time" to be part of your Birth Story, trust me on this one.

Dad Tip #14: Figure out your "Code Words" for Red Light, Yellow Light, Green Light and start practicing them now. "Code Words? Uh, what are you talking about?" I'm talking about you and Mama figuring out some low-key Code Words to use in front of other people to subtly help you both get on the same page about when things are good (green light), when they start to need to wrap up soon (yellow light), and when they need to be shut down as soon as possible (red light). Your now-very-pregnant partner will likely at times have extremely limited energy for small talk with neighbors, chats with total strangers about her giant belly, and/or interest in staying at a friend's dinner party much past 8pm. A great way to for you to continue to move into the Dad Zone, *better connect* to Mama during these last weeks of pregnancy, and *better prepare* for the post-baby chaos and influx of visitors into your home is to develop your own set of Code Words to use with each other when checking in on her fluctuating energy levels and interests. My wife and I settled on Avocado for green light, Lemon for yellow, and Tomato for red. Here's a few examples of how we put the Code Words to use;

Scene 1 – We are out for an early dinner with friends we hadn't seen in a while. My wife, in her 38th week of the pregnancy, was excited and feeling up for that outing earlier in the day, but as dinner went on, she started feeling extra tired and just wanted to go home and rest. Rather than suddenly blurting out loud "hey, I don't feel great, we need to leave pretty soon", thereby creating a bit of confusion in myself and our friends about how fast we need to wrap up and/or if she was going into labor or something, she just casually pinched my leg under the table as she asked the waiter for some *lemon* for her water. I got her drift and within a few minutes had told our friends that we actually needed to skip dessert and get back home so that Jenn could get some extra rest. Everything was cool, my wife wasn't left feeling like the party pooper for needing to cut things short, and I got to look like the *helpful and supportive* caring husband. Win-win, *$ka-ching$.*

Scene 2 – We had walked up to the aforementioned ice cream shop a few blocks from our house one evening for a tasty desert. My wife was now 40 weeks pregnant, feeling HUGE and uncomfortable and generally not happy with pretty much anything other than the thought of chocolate ice cream with some strawberries on it. Not being the pregnant one, I was doing great, but also somewhat oblivious to her degree of discomfort (not unusual ☺). We got to the ice cream shop and saw a medium length line of about 20 people in front of us, not surprising because it was a hot August evening in

Omaha. An older couple got in line behind us and started trying to chat with us, beginning with "Oh dear, I hope you don't have that baby right here in the ice cream shop!" I thought that was kind of funny and chuckled as I replied "Me too! I don't want to wait in line for 30 minutes and then not get any ice cream out of the deal." They thought that was quite humorous, but one look at Jenn made it pretty clear that she was NOT AMUSED with any of it. I quickly regrouped, gathered my thoughts and said, "Hey babe, why don't you just grab a seat on that bench in the shade across the street and put together our grocery list while I get our ice cream. I know we need *tomatoes* for sure, but I'll think about what else we might need while I wait in line for both of us." She glared at me a second, thinking that I was maybe putting her in time-out or something, but then got my drift and softly said, "oh, right, *tomatoes*, good idea babe" and happily went over to the bench, off her feet, and out of the spotlight, while I chit-chatted with the older couple about silly baby names until I got our ice cream. Win-win, *$ka-ching$!*

Scene 3 – We had been out at the neighborhood pool for an early evening dip and we were just drying off and packing up to head back home when some friends walked in. Jenn had just mentioned to me that she wasn't feeling all that great, so as the friends were walking up to us to say "hi" I immediately mentioned to them that it was too bad we couldn't stay any longer and we were on our way out. Jenn then said "hey babe, do you know if we have any *avocados* at home? I want to make some fresh guacamole later on when we leave." She then turned to our friends and told them how nice it was to see them, etc.... I paused, confused for a second, then remembered the Code Words and shifted my conversation to how I too was glad they walked in and would actually love to visit with them for a little while before we head home. Win-win, *$ka-ching$*.

These all are some easy examples where one of us dropping a quick Code Word helped us both stay on the same page about my wife's changing mood and energy, and allowed me to help adjust our circumstances to match them more easily than I would have otherwise. Of course, my wife is a grown-ass woman and is more than capable of speaking up directly in the above circumstances, and any other that we might be in as well. However, very pregnant ladies (and brand-new Mamas!) are often tired of being the "bad guy" and always wanting to go home early, sit on benches by themselves, or answer questions about how their mood and energy can shift so quickly. These Code Words allow you to move further into the Dad Zone, be *better connected* to Mama, and work as a team in social circumstances, all things that will be MUCH more important after Baby comes in a few weeks!

Dad Tip #15: Watch at least 3 hi-def 1080p "Birth Videos" with your pregnant partner, including at least one C-section. Your child's impending birth is going to be pretty dramatic, no matter how things go down. You need to be *better prepared* for all the possible sights and sounds that come with it so that it doesn't become *traumatic* too! The short version of what you might need to prepare for is that the sexy vagina that you are used to is going to transform itself into the birth canal, and that's a very different beast! Your normally cool, calm, and collected partner may also transform into a different beast too, so sitting down together (*better connected!*) to watch some cool birth videos will help you both get a better sense of how things are going to look, literally and figuratively. A word of caution here, childbirth is a pretty intense biological event, so if you are particularly squeamish about such things then perhaps skipping this Dad Tip altogether is your best plan. Read on to see what I mean...

Quick anecdote on this **Dad Tip**: A buddy of mine who had a kid 4 years ago and, therefore, did not get a chance to read ***WTF***'s **D15 (Birth Video)**, was doing OK all through Labor, holding his wife's hand and telling her she was amazing. However, things took a dark turn for him when the attending OB asked him if he wanted to see the baby's head starting to come out. He casually moved to the foot of the bed, looked at his baby's head coming out (covered in blood and who knows what), and promptly fainted right there on the spot! One of the attending nurses had to quickly grab him on his way down and then help him over to a chair, causing a pretty big commotion in the process. His wife immediately started freaking out, wondering if the sudden chaos was about something being drastically wrong with the baby. Needless to say, that Birth Story did not entirely feature him as the Hero he could have been... Remember the motto of this book – *better connected, better prepared!*

Although the 3rd Trimester technically ends when Baby is born, we are going to wrap up our coverage here and leave "Labor and Delivery" as its own subsequent chapter. As I mentioned at the beginning of the book, your role as Dad is one that that steadily increases throughout the pregnancy but then jumps into super-turbo-overdrive once your partner goes into labor. Like with our rollercoaster analogy, that trek up the first hill slowly gets more intense and suspenseful, but then that fall down the other side is where the real ride begins. Each chapter here so far has gotten progressively longer and more detailed and complicated as we've tracked Mama's pregnancy, and your evolving role in it, up that hill. You have been an important and integral part of this pregnancy journey, but honestly, what you've done up until the real labor begins is all small potatoes. Which is probably a good thing for most guys, truth be told. However, all the good Dad Zone work you've been doing so far in getting *better connected* to your partner and *better prepared* for what lies ahead is going to start to pay off for *everybody* in the next chapter once the contractions start getting serious.

Chapter 4 Summary for You: Continuing to build on our foundational **Big Ideas** and the 1st and 2nd Trimester **Dad Tips**, this chapter filled up pretty quickly with more **Dad Tips** for specific things for you to do now to get *better connected* to Mama and *better prepared* for Baby.

D8 (Due Date) has you shifting your language (and Mama's thinking) off the specific "Due Date" and on to a more general and accurate "Expected Arrival" window of time. We then got more specific with **D9 (Gift Tracker)** for the Gift Tracker Spreadsheet (GTS) and the **D10 (Top 10)** for the Top Ten must haves list for Dads. The birth place field trip covered in **D11 (Field Trip)** focuses on parking and other things that are different when you have a laboring Mama with you. We hit the Go Bag essentials in **D12 (Go Bag)**, and went over the basics of the Birth Plan in **D13 (Birth Plan)**. Clear communication is crucial, as covered in **D14 (Code Words)**, and your final *better prepared* action is to watch a few real-life birth videos in all their bloody glory as recommended by **D15 (Birth Video)**. Get ready man, shit's about to get real when Mama goes into Labor, coming up next!

Chapter 4 Summary for Mama: This 3rd Trimester has things accelerating rapidly for you and Baby, and for Dad too. Hopefully by this point he is at least coming up to a reasonable speed in the *helpful and supportive* department. We covered a bunch of things for him in this chapter to help bring him further along, specifically getting him more involved in some of the particular preparations for Baby coming. We also reminded him that Baby will come when Baby is ready and to not get overly focused on an exact due date as that only adds to your anxiety. We touched upon him helping you keep track of all the Baby Shower gifts, and suggested that you take a family field trip or two over to your hospital or anticipated birth place to get better acquainted with parking, the building lay-out, and other things you don't want to have to guess about when you are in Active Labor. We covered the Go Bag and how he should have that ready to go by week 37, as well as having your Birth Plan in place by then too.

On the fun side, we also recommended that you both figure out some cool Code Words for the two of you to practice using now to make navigating tricky social situations a little easier. These Code Words essentially cover Red light, Yellow light, and Green light communications and are meant to be a secret shorthand way for you both to be on the same page about your fluctuating energies and degrees of interest in whatever is going on in the moment. Many Mamas have limited social energy available by now, but still want to try to hang out with friends and continue some pre-pregnancy habits like staying awake past 8pm. These Code Words can help Dad keep track of how you are feeling and can help him figure out how to be a good teammate and work with you in helping to manage these social situations. Help him help you by trying to track and anticipate your fluctuating energies and emotional needs and then use your Code Words accordingly. Remember, most guys are not very good at interpreting a "subtle look" from across the room, or even across the table. These Code Words will make both your lives easier, please use them! Finally, we suggested that you sit down and watch a few birth videos together to get more comfortable for Baby's upcoming arrival. Specifically, he has probably never seen a vagina in its natural state of giving birth to a baby, so you want that first, and potentially shocking, moment for him to be associated with somebody else's vagina, not yours. Trust me on this one.

Chapter 5
Labor & Delivery

The Time is Now!

Welcome to THE defining event that kicks off your new life as a family, starting when the first pangs of labor start to come on strong, and continuing on over who knows how many hours until you are happily and dazedly actually holding Baby in your arms. All of the things that happen during this time period to you, Mama, and Baby, are going to be locked into memory forever as the founding narrative of your new life, and therefore need to be understood in their utmost importance, specifically for you and your role in what will be known forever onward as the "Birth Story." Everything that follows in this chapter will be presented as information specifically detailed to help you be the most awesome *helpful and supportive* Dad possible here. And keep in mind that all of *that* is just so that Mama and Baby can have the best possible birth experience, so let's jump right into to the big picture idea of the "Birth Story" before getting any further into the step by step details.

Big Idea # 9: The "Birth Story" is going to be the biggest narrative in your and Mama's lives for a *long* time. It is Mama's story of the birthing of her baby, of finally and fully becoming a Mom – starting from the early pangs of labor and going through the trials and travails of delivery. This story climaxes when she finally gets to meet Baby and holds them in her arms, and usually winds down with the less important details covering your remaining stay in the birthing place until you get back home. Please remember, she has been waiting and wanting to meet her baby for *almost a full year* now, and this event is the biggest moment of her life so far as covered in **B4 (Biggest Deal)**. Many a Dad I have worked with in my workshop has totally and completely underestimated the importance of his role in this situation and has then had to regrettably sit through countless retellings of how "and then he just left me there *laboring by myself* on the curb for 15 minutes while he went to find a parking spot!", or "he said he was hungry and left me laboring for an hour *by myself* while he went to go get lunch at the café," or "he said he didn't feel well and then went to go puke in the bathroom for 20 minutes while I was just lying there *by myself* screaming at the top of my lungs trying to push the baby out!"

These things all happened to Dads I know, and really cost these guys huge points in EVERY category of their relationship. Now compare those events seared into the memory of those particular Mama's brains with these other examples, equally seared into the permanent record of these Dads: "He was TOTALLY AMAZING. He kept calm the whole time, held my hand, and told me how much he believed in me," and "he really showed up for me 100%. Any lingering doubts I may have had about whether or not he was ready to be a Dad dissolved instantly when I saw how *helpful and supportive* he was from the first moment labor really kicked in," and "I have never felt so loved by him as I did when he was right there by my side the whole time I was pushing the baby out. He was my hero." See the theme there? *Better connected* to Mama, and *better prepared* for Baby's arrival. So, which dude do you want to be?

Now that we have the basic timeline of what's covered in the "Birth Story," we can start to get into the specifics of how this is all going to go down. This chapter might feel a bit long and complex, but that is just because having a baby can be a pretty intense ordeal, even for you as the "passive observer." I'll try to keep things moving along though, and will particularly push hard on giving you specific tips spelling out exactly what you can do to be more of an "active participant" at each step along the way.

Note: This chapter is written for those choosing to go the more natural childbirth route of Baby comes out when Baby is ready. As in, you're not sure when it's going to happen or if it's even really happening when it starts. The timing for this path is highly variable and very uncertain. Alternative scenarios have a set time and date and include a scheduled induction, where Mama is scheduled to be induced into labor via artificial means, and a scheduled C-section, where Mama is scheduled for a surgical C-section to get Baby out. Both of these alternatives remove the uncertainty and chaos around the timing of home laboring and all that comes with that, so if your family plan calls for either of those choices then some of what follows may not apply to your situation. Still, read it all anyway! Some Babies don't care that you have them scheduled to come out at 10am on the 15th and might just decide to show up unannounced at midnight on the 13th. Remember, *better prepared* is half of our big picture motto here in ***WTF***!

Let's start with a quick and simple overview showing how many pregnant couples imagine things tend to work regarding labor and delivery, based on what they've seen and heard on TV and the movies:

1) Contractions start and then intensify
2) Her "water" breaks
3) You immediately rush off to the hospital in a panic
4) After some yelling and pushing, she has the baby
5) You go back home the next day

Seems pretty straightforward, eh? And perhaps an extremely small number of births pretty closely follow the steps described above. However, like most things, the lived reality is often *much* different than how any simple description tells it, and there are many possible wrinkles and permutations in and between each of the above steps. Therefore, I'll give you a quick overview of how labor *actually* works inside the woman's body, and then we can jump right into your role in the process. But first let's circle back to **B5 (Anxiety)** and its power as that is both largely unavoidable here and one of the biggest things we are going to try to manage with our various efforts and actions during this time. The anxiety that comes with simply being pregnant is fundamentally dwarfed both in intensity and impact for Mama as compared to the potential anxiety that comes with the actual birthing of Baby. Managing and lessening that anxiety is the golden ticket for a better experience for you, Mama, and Baby. This is absolutely HUGE, so let's look into it a bit closer to understand why.

Many of the most common misconceptions about childbirth in general is that it must necessarily be full of strife and struggle. Most TV and movie depictions of childbirth are loud, messy, and chockfull of drama. You know why? Drama sells, screaming sells, and anxiety of all kinds sells. Annoying and unfortunate, but true. The fact of the matter is that childbirth throughout the rest of the animal kingdom is often a surprisingly calm and silent affair. The mama zebra or buffalo or whatever most often just sort of drifts off to a secluded and safe space and goes about having their baby without a bunch of screaming and yelling from 15 other zebras all standing around yelling "PUSH!!!" at the top of their lungs. In fact, many women who subscribe to more of the "natural childbirth" philosophical approach and attempt to mimic more natural circumstances (warm, cozy, dark, quiet) are often able to "get through" childbirth with a minimum of discomfort and yelling and screaming. How? By the *intentional cultivation of a non-anxious state for Mama*, primarily aided with tremendous assistance from YOU, the Dad.

Big Idea #10: Your mantra here is Be Attentive, Be Calm, Be Competent. Anxiety, hers and yours, is the number one impediment to a smooth (as possible) Labor & Delivery. We need to step into a little science here to help you understand the *huge* importance of minimizing her anxiety from the first signs of Labor commencing onward. The main birth hormone coursing through Mama's body is Oxytocin. Also popularly known as the "Love Hormone," for women it is involved in sexual arousal, recognition, trust, and mother-infant bonding. In laboring women Oxytocin is also the singular biggest driver of contractions and the other underlying uterine muscle movements, and also in stimulating lactation after Baby is born. Oxytocin both creates and flows freely in states of calmness, trust, and with somebody well known (like you). Hence, doing your part to create the ideal circumstances to allow the Oxytocin to flow as freely as possible is, in my opinion, the absolute #1 job you have right now as the baby Dada, and *everything* that follows in this chapter is an explanation or exploration of how to do just that.

On the other side of the chemistry coin is Adrenaline, the fight or flight hormone, triggered by fear and anxiety. That hormone literally stops Oxytocin in its tracks, slowing or stalling Labor completely. Imagine our friend the zebra is happily and quietly getting ready to have her baby in the bushes, but then suddenly hears some lions roaring and getting closer. Full Stop. Anxiety shuts down Oxytocin. No baby coming out right now. So, her labor stops and she jumps up and quickly rejoins the nearby herd until the danger passes and she feels safe again, at which point she'll head back over to the bushes to have her baby. Your partner is obviously no zebra, and there are no lions roaring (ideally), but any fear and anxiety she has will indeed act directly *against* her Oxytocin and her "natural" Labor.

Remember how HUGE this moment is her life from **B4 (Biggest Deal),** and how much time and energy she has spent worrying about it from **B5 (Anxiety).** All of that energy is going to be coming up to the surface now as she feels Baby making their way out into the world. Stress, tension, fear, and anxiety will almost certainly be present in some degree throughout her Labor and birth of Baby, but there are many things you can do to help alleviate much of it. Oxytocin is the antidote to that stuff, and you are the main agent to help stimulate that hormone's flow as those things rise up. Holding her hand, looking into her eyes with love and compassion, and providing calming assurances and encouragement all boost her Oxytocin levels.

More Oxytocin means less stress for Mama, and less stress for Mama translates into a better experience for everybody. Therefore, you *must* understand the importance of this particular **Big Idea** and do your *absolute best* to help her remain focused on you. You do this by remaining focused on her (Attentive), through your relaxing presence (Calmness), and through your helpful words and actions (Competence). This is your new mantra from this point forward – **Be Attentive, Be Calm, Be Competent**. Doing so will help her, and Baby, have the best childbirth possible and will cement your role as the helpful Hero in her "Birth Story."

- **Be Attentive** by keeping track of Mama and the overall birth process and where you are in it at all times so that you can modify your supporting actions accordingly. UNDER NO CIRCUMSTANCES should you be tempted to dive into your phone/computer and be scrolling through your social media, playing video games, or checking your work emails, regardless of how chill circumstances may seem to be on the surface of things. She is literally *having a baby* in front of you, pay attention only to her!
- **Be Calm** at all times. No matter how stressed or panicked you are in any given moment, being calm and composed puts you in the best position to make good decisions and to be a safe and steadying influence on Mama. All of your preplanning should get you to the birth center or hospital or wherever in good shape, and once there you turn over the biggest roles to

the professionals. Here is also where having your **D7 (Doula)** as your wingman is priceless.

- **Be Competent** in your role here. As we have gone over before, your preplanning activities such as the site-visit **D11 (Field Trip),** the **D12 (Go Bag),** and the **D13 (Birth Plan)** should free up most of your attention to be solely focused on your partner, where it absolutely should be. Fumbling around at home in the dark looking for your computer charger while your partner is doubled over in labor pain is not a good look for you. Neither is yelling frantically for a doctor as soon as you walk into the hospital. Have a plan, work the plan.

Again, ideally you have laid a solid foundation in the above department by taking a **D6 (Birth Class)** of some sort and have discussed and planned for your delivery comfort options as part of your **D13 (Birth Plan).** However, if you've actually done nothing at all and you suddenly find yourself reading this chapter in a panic in the bathroom of the delivery room, that's cool too. Just sit next to Mama, hold her hand, look into her eyes, tell her how amazing she is, and offer her sips of water. Many couples have planned for various other comfort mechanisms such as calming music, favorite pillows and/or blankets, massage oil, ambient lighting, meditation mantras, essential oils, and innumerable other things. These should all be in your Birth Plan and your "Go Bag", but in the end what she needs most is the emotional rock of her attentive, calm, and competent partner and soon-to-be-Dad dude right there by her side.

There are obviously lots of potential wrinkles and permutations in birthing circumstances that will make doing all of the above challenging at many points in the process, and we'll cover the most common ones below. However, your mantra of "**Be Attentive, Be Calm, Be Competent**" all throughout the labor and delivery should help guide you in whatever situation you're facing. The **B9 (Birth**

Story) is going to stick with you both forever, make sure your role in it is something that brings you both pride and joy.

Actual Stages of Childbirth

Now to the *actual* stages of childbirth, not the 5 "common sense" as-seen-on-TV steps that started this chapter. Assuming that Baby is full term and otherwise ready to go, the childbirth process is usually broken down into 3 basic stages. Stage 1 is labor, Stage 2 is from full cervical dilation to the actual delivery of the baby, and Stage 3 is the delivery of the placenta. We'll cover each of these in some detail below, but I'll also break things down a bit further later on in order to focus on giving you specific tips on how you can be an All-Star Dad at the various points along the way.

Labor is Stage 1 and covers the process of Mama's body changing its job from keeping Baby in to getting ready to push Baby out. It is usually further divided into 3 subphases - Early Labor, Active Labor, and the Transition. FYI, "Contraction" is the word used to describe the work that the cervical muscles are doing here in Labor to open up the bottom of the uterus. The uterus has essentially been locked closed for the past 9 months, so pulling it open can be quite a lot of work for these little cervical muscles, especially since they haven't ever done this before. Imagine if you never did any bicep curls but then were asked to do several hundred reps over many hours. That would probably be very crampy and painful, especially at the end, right? That's somewhat like what is happening here in labor.

Early Labor is when these contraction reps first begin and before they start to intensify and become more regularly spaced apart. This milder "warm up" phase can last for a few hours or up to several days and can usually be "enjoyed" in the comfort of one's home. You'll probably want to call your Doula/OB/birth center/hospital and let them know what's going on when this starts, but generally this is a time for both you and Mama to mainly practice relaxing, taking deep breaths, easy walks, and hot baths/showers. It's also a good time to make sure you have copies of your Birth Plan printed out for the birth team, the Go Bag finalized, your pet sitting plan finalized, and main contact person brought into the loop.

The second phase is known as Active Labor and is characterized by an intensification in timing and frequency of contractions. This is usually when you should grab your Go-Bag and head out to your birth destination, remembering to text a status update to your point person from your Birth Plan on your way out the door. Your focus here should be on helping Mama stay as physically and emotionally comfortable as possible during this phase. Changing laboring positions, taking a shower/bath, and going for short, assisted walks around the maternity ward are all good ideas here.

The final phase of labor is the Transition and is both the most intense and (thankfully) shortest of the three phases. Contractions will now be coming on almost constantly with very brief pauses in between. Mama will likely be very focused and uncomfortable during this stage. You need to watch for this and tone down pretty much everything but hand holding, gentle touching, and encouraging words.

Stage 2 of the birth process is when Baby exits the womb through the cervical opening and makes their way down through the birth canal and out into the world. This stage can be very intense and vary from 20 minutes or less up to 2 hours or more. This is the scene that most movies and TV shows cover where the Mom is sweating and crying and screaming out obscenities. There will be lots of coaching from the delivery team, alternating between active pushing and moments of resting in between. Your partner may surprise you with her energy and expression here, including her fluency and skill in using the f-bomb in general and at you in particular. Don't worry, you'll probably be laughing about it later. Your role here is to be Chief Encourager, mainly by holding her hands, looking into her eyes, and telling her how awesome and inspiring she is in between pushes. The hardest part for her will be the "crowning" of the baby's head through her vaginal opening, but once the head clears the baby will pretty much do a quick half turn and then pop right out. Congrats Mom and Dad!! Hopefully you followed my **D15 (Birth Video)** recommendation from the last chapter and watched multiple videos of childbirth so that you are prepared for this last dramatic moment and remain cool, calm, and composed throughout the process. Congratulations, you are now officially a Dad!

But wait, we aren't quite finished. Stage 3 of childbirth is the delivery of the placenta. This is the shortest stage and often even seems like almost an afterthought now that Baby is here in your arms. The placenta usually pretty much comes out on its own after a few more series of mild contractions, but often the doctor or birth attendants will help it along with mild tugging on the remaining umbilical cord and with massaging of Mama's belly. After the placenta comes out Mama will be closely monitored to make sure that her uterus continues to contract back down and that there are no ongoing bleeding concerns, post-delivery issues, or other complications. Your role here is just to remain physically and emotionally present, hold her and your baby, and whisper "you're amazing" to her over and over again.

So that's the basic, high-level overview of your standard textbook childbirth process. We'll now slowly walk back through it again, tying your Birth Plan and preparation more directly to what's going down in each stage, and specifically focusing on *your* role in the process.

Stage 1, Phase 1 – Early Labor

As we covered above, Early Labor is when Mama's body starts its final preparations for the birth of Baby and can last on average from 8 – 12 hours. Please keep in mind that this number and the rest of the timing ranges that I mention are just averages and may vary widely in both duration and intensity for your situation. Imagine this phase as analogous to the warming up and stretching that takes place on a ballfield before the game starts. Players are moving around, doing short sprints, some high knee drills, maybe some extra hamstring and quad warm-ups as the clock is ticking down to game time. Mama's body is doing essentially the same thing and is "warming up" for having a baby. Her contractions are starting to feel a little stronger, last a little longer, and happen a little more regularly. This is when you turn to your new mantra: **Be Attentive, Be Calm, Be Competent.**

Be Attentive by looking out for the commencement and progress of your partner's contractions. She'll probably already have experienced Braxton-Hicks practice contractions on and off for several weeks now as her body has started to prepare for the big event. Many women may also end up having several short episodes of more intense contractions here and there in the final few days of pregnancy. All these contractions are very real when they are happening, so you may end up having what turns out to be a "false start" or three if the contractions taper off shortly after they start, but you won't know in the moment where they are going to go. Therefore, you want to be emotionally present and attentive for any and all contractions. Remember, what you are actually monitoring is the *intensification* and *timing* of the contractions to let you know when it is time to go to the hospital or birth center. There are plenty of good apps that will help you time and plot out the contractions, just make sure you already have one on your phone by now and know how to use it! You can also offer her some water, a snack, or to put on some music she likes. Lots of options here. Just don't say something like, "well, wake me up again when you're sure that it's the real thing" if she starts having contractions at 3 AM for the 2nd night in a row. I did exactly that with our first pregnancy, and I still hear about it occasionally to this day. Dud Zone alert!

Be Calm by trying to strike the perfect balance of excitedly happy and serenely relaxed. You'll go back and forth from both ends, but when possible try to time your swing in whatever direction bests helps you *better connect* to Mama and helps to keep her grounded. You can also hit her with some more **B6 (Mom Comms)** and remind her of how strong she is and how she has done such an amazing job of taking care of the baby so far. Additionally, you can strategically tell her how glad you are that you have (ideally) attended a **D6 (Birth Class)**, hired your awesome **D7 (Doula),** and watched all those **D15 (Birth Videos)** together. Now's also a good time to suggest that you do some of your favorite down-time things together, such as going for a walk to get ice cream, playing whatever card or board games you like, or adding a couple last minute dinner or dessert options to your fridge. This time is all about *better connecting* and showing Mama that you are committed to **B8 (Team Work)** and "teaming up" together with her for the upcoming journey, so look for things to do together that show her that you are right there with her as a steadying and calming influence.

Be Competent by identifying and staying ahead of anything tangible that she might be worried about. You've already done most of the legwork here over the last few weeks with your various **Dad Tips** covering the Birth Plan, Go Bag, route planning, birth site visits, and proper Baby car seat installation. Now's a good time to simply talk through each of those things again with her briefly, specifically focusing on how you two have been working together and "teaming up" as much as possible all this time and that you will continue to do so here with Baby's imminent arrival. Remind her of how you guys are all set and ready to head out to the birth destination as soon as the right signs are there, and that now the best thing, for both of you, is to take deep breaths and relax to help save up your energy for what lies ahead – you'll need it.

Stage 1, Phase 2 – Active Labor

To recap from earlier, you are moving into Active Labor when the contractions become more regular and intensify in both frequency and duration. A good general rule to follow is the "3-2-1 Rule" where the contractions are roughly 3 minutes apart, have been so for 2 hours, and last about 1 minute each. But in order to know when you get to this point you will need to have been diligently timing and tracking her contractions throughout this whole process. Once you hit "3-2-1" then that is a good time to head out to your birth destination and get checked in and settled into your room. Before we go any further here, it's time for another **Dad Tip**:

Dad Tip #16: Her "water breaking" is NOT AN EMERGENCY. Contrary to pretty much every depiction of somebody's "water breaking" on TV or the movies, you DO NOT need to immediately panic and run about like a maniac prior to sprinting to the car and racing to the hospital. Generally speaking, most OB's want Baby's delivery to occur within 24 hours of the "water breaking", so that is the actual time window you are working with here, not ASAP. So, barring any extreme pain or active bleeding by Mama, the "water breaking" moment should just be documented as a point of reference to be discussed later with the birth attendants during the routine check-in and intake process. In fact, for many women the "water breaking" often doesn't occur until later on in labor, or even until the baby is actually coming out! Even cooler is when babies are born "en caul," which refers to the baby coming out still enclosed in a fully intact amniotic sac. Whoa! Pretty amazing and worth a Google search to see for yourself if you're curious. Basic lesson here with the whole "water breaking" thing - don't act like anybody in a made-for-TV drama! Come to think of it, pretty much never act like them in *any* situation, but *especially* not here.

Getting back to our discussion of Active Labor, this phase is often when both you and Mama are probably each having your own revelation of "Oh, shit! This is actually happening now! WE'RE HAVING A BABY!" Mama will likely be simultaneously the most excited you have ever seen her and also the most terrified that you have ever seen her. She's finally about to meet her baby after months and month of waiting, yet still has to go through what could be the single most arduous challenge she has ever faced in order to do so. She'll be in this Active Labor phase for on average from 3 – 5 hours before she gets to the Transition, the next level up in the process. Your job here in Active Labor, again, is to **Be Attentive, Be Calm, Be Competent**.

Be Attentive to her ever shifting moods and comfort levels so that you can tailor your actions and plans accordingly. Watch her face for signs of pain and discomfort, pay attention to her grip strength when holding her hand, give her some emotional and psychological space by not overly engaging her with lots of questions, jokes, or stories, and do your best to remain patiently attentive.

Be Calm by staying deeply grounded in your role here as her main support person. Feel free to join her in her moments of excitement and anticipation, but absolutely do not join her in her moments of worry and panic. The best thing to do when these arise for Mama is to acknowledge how scary this might feel right now, and give her some space to process it a little bit. Then slowly try to reorient her away from the fear and remind her of how amazing it is going to be to finally hold her baby here shortly and how she has been working so hard to prepare for this moment. You need to be that emotionally rock steady "safe place" for her to lean into from here onwards. Some good phrases for you to say here include "I'm right here with you" and "you're amazing."

Be Competent by using all the supportive partner tricks and techniques you learned in your Birth Class and elsewhere. Talk about how she has done such a good job preparing for this moment, and mention that even though it probably all feels a bit scary, that you and the birth team are right here with her. You can also remind her to focus on deep and even breathing, helping her change positions as often as necessary, offering water and ice chips, rubbing her lower back and shoulders, and telling her she is amazing, beautiful, and your hero too.

Stage 1, Phase 3 – The Transition

The Transition is indeed a tricky phase and can manifest very differently for many women. It is the "transition" between Laboring and actually pushing the baby out and is the shortest phase, averaging from 30 min to 2 hours for most women. Contractions here can be almost happening one right after another, with only brief resting points in between. Your partner really needs you the most right here, even if she appears to be not actually responding to you, or even aware of your presence. Many women report an almost "animal instinct" element taking over here as their body makes its final adjustments to prepare for Baby to enter the birth canal. They often talk about feeling slightly detached from the process and therefore are not really able or interested in responding to any small talk or overt engagement from you or the other birth attendants. This is also the phase where some Birth Stories will have the women yelling and screaming at the man about this all being his fault (for getting her pregnant) or blowing up at him for trying to "lighten the mood" by cracking jokes. Remember, NOTHING is funny in the Transition.

Be Attentive to Mama's physical comfort and positioning, but also try to track her emotional state, noting that when she starts to get withdrawn and serious that you are now entering the Transition. At this point you now need to be listening to the OB, Doula, and/or midwife and watching your partner to make sure she is following their instructions and/or answering their questions.

Be Calm because everybody else around you will be working pretty hard. Mama isn't at the final pushing stage yet, but this is a very busy and active phase for everybody because Baby will be coming out into the world very soon. Your calmness may be the only beacon in the sea for Mama as she is struggling with the pounding waves of contractions.

Be Competent by giving her lots of loving looks into her eyes, hand holding, and reassuring words, but don't overdo it. Mama is in her own world here and often can't even hear what anybody is saying. Your simple loving presence by her side, hand in hand, may just be the best thing you can offer.

Stage 2 – Through the birth canal and into the real world

Once the cervix fully dilates to approximately 10cm (which is 4 inches across, about the width of your palm) then the baby can begin its trip down the birth canal and out into the world. This trip can be over in just a few minutes or might take a few hours, but no matter what will be the most energetic for everybody involved. Mama will be alternating between pushing really hard to help Baby move along and then resting in between pushes because she might be pretty exhausted by now. The attending baby team will also be very engaged in coaching Mama on her pushes and keeping track of the baby's progress and vital signs. There might now be extra people in the room too, such as medical residents and extra nurses getting ready to help Baby once they emerge.

When Baby's head reaches the vaginal opening that's called "crowning" and is very exciting for everybody. It's also known as the

"Ring of Fire," because that's exactly what it feels like to many a Mama as Baby's head comes out. Exciting indeed! Some women report how using a mirror to help them see Baby's head at this time gives them extra inspiration and strength to continue, so be ready to assist in that process if needed. After Baby's head clears the vaginal opening then the rest of the body usually comes out pretty quickly and easily. There is often a decent amount of amniotic fluid and other stuff that all comes out with the baby, so be prepared for that as a possibility. **D15 (Birth Video)** suggested watching multiple birth videos to get you trained up for all the action you are about to see here, so be ready.

Be Attentive to what Mama is saying and needing, as well as to what the birth professionals are asking of you and her. While obviously action-packed for Mama, this stage can be a hectic time for you too. You will likely be very active here, doing a variety of things to help Mama get through this final, challenging stage. Mama will be fully engaged in the birthing process and can use all the encouragement and faith you can offer because this may be the hardest part of the hardest thing she has ever done.

Be Calm, no matter what is happening, because that is exactly what your partner needs from you. Many women report the Dad as being the only person she could even hear or see during this stage. Her spotlight may be entirely on you, so be the calm, steady person she needs you to be here.

Be Competent by helping hold her hand or even a leg when she is pushing, and by giving her lots of encouraging words about being "almost there" and "you're so beautiful" and "our baby is almost out." You need to stay steady and present and focused entirely on Mama and your job through the entire crowning and actual emergence of the baby, i.e., no "yuck" faces or saying things like "damn, that gotta hurt!" or passing out at the sight of all that blood and stuff. Speaking of funny faces:

Dad Tip #17: Your baby might look a little weird when they first come out, do not freak out! Think about it for a minute. Your baby has been in a warm, dark, watery environment for the past 9 months and then just got squished and squeezed and pushed out of the tight confines of the birth canal. Therefore, many babies come out with some or all of the following – cone-shaped head, swollen eyelids, swollen genitals, various splotches of color or pigmentation, vernix coating (a white, cheesy substance), and/or lanugo (a fine downy hair). You'll likely be overwhelmed with joy and fatigue and amazement and will be so happy to see your baby that none of this will directly register as a concern. However, I've definitely heard some stories of some Dads that have been startled or overwhelmed by how "alien" their baby looked when they first came out. Hopefully you've prepared yourself by watching plenty of birth videos and seen a few brand-new babies and will be ready for pretty much anything at this point. Within a short while your baby will have been cleaned up and wrapped up and given a cute little hat to keep its head warm and will look just as cute as a button.

Back to the birth process, the instant Baby fully pops out is obviously a big deal and a lot of things will be happening in a short period of time. Your birth professional will officially call the time and immediately start to do a quick health check up on the baby, focusing on skin tone, color, and other signs that the baby has arrived in a healthy state (this is called the APGAR, Google it if you are into the details of these things). Your **D13 (Birth Plan)** should have a good chunk of space devoted to these few minutes, including possible requests for immediate skin-to-skin with Mama, delayed umbilical cord clamping and/or cord blood banking, delayed baby wiping/cleaning, having Dad (you) be the one to cut the cord, and several other areas of family preferences. Assuming everything looks good with Baby during this first quick once-over, they might then place Baby right on Mama's chest for some important sustained skin-to-skin contact while they ensure the placenta is safely birthed in Stage 3. But before we get to Stage 3, we need to cover one more thing:

Dad Tip #18: Know how to hold your brand-new baby! I can't tell you how many Dads I know who literally almost passed out in fear when they were asked if they were ready to hold their baby – "Uh, no, not at all!" Don't be one of those guys. The most basic rule when holding a new baby, especially when receiving Baby from or passing Baby to somebody else, is to remember that this whole process involves a chest-to-chest transfer. It is NOT an extended arm, here-you-go kind of move. Later, after you get home and get more comfortable, you can move to some of the more popular holds, such as the "football" or "belly flop", but for Day 1 we are going to 100% go with the basic cradle hold. This standard cradle hold is a particularly good move for tightly swaddled newborns because your left elbow crook is the perfect spot for resting this little living lump of cuteness.

Here's a quick tutorial on the cradle hold. Most people will tend to hold a baby with its head resting against the left side of the chest, likely due to an instinctive awareness of the comfort the baby gets by hearing and feeling the heartbeat this way. Therefore, the best way to pass/receive a baby is to stand side-by-side with the other person, not facing each other. Side-by-side allows a much easier transfer of the baby with minimal turning and reversing hands and such, and also allows the baby's head to remain fully supported the whole time. When receiving the baby, allow the passer to place the baby's head with their left hand into your waiting-for-baby cradled left arm. As the passer pushes the baby's bum into your arm you can then scoop your right arm under to complete the hand-off. You are now standing with the baby fully cradled in your arms, head elevated and resting against your body.

Don't forget, always keep the baby's head *fully* supported! This can often be best accomplished by having your right arm cradled under the left far enough that your right hand is up in front of the baby's head, ready to support it when you need to move around, sit down, or stand up. When you are ready to pass the baby back to Mama, or to Grammy or whoever, get side-to-side with them first. With your right arm fully underneath and supporting Baby, slide your left arm/elbow back, allowing your left hand to move to under the baby's head. With Baby's head fully supported by your left hand and its body/bum fully supported by your right hand, you can gently push and place the baby into the recipients waiting left arm cradle. As they get their arms in the proper position you can then slide your right arm right back out. Congrats, you did it! It's a good idea to practice both the holding and passing/receiving of Baby with a doll or something at home a few times before your first live opportunity, preferably with Mama as your assistant – doing this is a *better connected, better prepared* home run and earns you huge Dad Card credits too. Win-win, *$ka-ching$!*

Finally, speaking of Baby's head, I need to tell you about something that many Dads find to be a really weird situation – even weirder than the cone-shaped bit I already warned you about. The top front of Baby's head will have a big area underneath the skin or hair where it will be really soft and squishy, and there's another smaller soft spot on the back of the head too. Like, no underlying skull kind of soft and squishy. Don't worry, it's absolutely supposed to be this way so that Baby can more easily squeeze through the birth canal. Remember earlier when we mentioned how babies often come out with weirdly shaped heads? The skull's bone plates, or fontanelles, will grow together and fully close sometime between 9 and 18 months, but it can still be more than a bit disorienting to feel those soft spots on baby's head until then. Just a heads up on this one, and a reminder not to make any "ewwww" faces or crude remarks about it, well for at least the first day or two. ☺

Stage 3 – Delivery of the placenta

Often overlooked by expectant parents when thinking about childbirth, the placenta delivery is the shortest and last stage in the process, but one closely monitored by the medical team. Shortly after Baby is out the placenta will begin to detach from the wall of the uterus and be expelled through a series of mild contractions. As mentioned earlier, your birth attendants may assist this process by giving Mama an injection of a chemical contracting agent, like Pitocin, and by gently pulling on the remaining umbilical cord to help it along. Once the placenta is out of Mama it will then be measured and examined for its condition and health. Because placental detachment creates a wound in the uterus, Mama will be closely monitored at this stage to make sure that postpartum bleeding is within healthy limits and that any remaining medical needs, like the stitching up of minor tears, are resolved.

Many couples today opt to have the placenta saved and sent to a placenta encapsulation specialist. They will dehydrate and powder the placenta in order to turn the remains into pills to be taken by Mama over the next few months to help ward off Post-Partum Depression. The scientific jury is still out on the effectiveness of the practice, but it has many fans among new mothers, including my wife Jenn. And Post-Partum Depression is a very serious situation (which we'll cover in detail later as **Scary Moment #4**), so anything that helps minimize the chances of that occurring seems like a wise investment to me.

Finally, if you chose to have a Doula here with you during the childbirth then they will most likely be preparing to leave once the placenta is safely delivered. Many will briefly step out of the room to grab a cup of coffee or quick bite to eat to give you and your new family some time alone together. They'll then circle back to check in with you one last time to see if they can be of further service before saying goodbye. Doulas are the absolute best, and I will again *strongly* suggest **D7 (Doula)** and that you hire one to help your team have the best experience possible!

A quick final note on childbirth here is **Scary Moment #3: Things don't always follow the simple linear program of your Birth Plan.** Childbirth has become much safer in the last century, but it will never be risk-free. While the majority of hospital births are fairly routine and require minimal medical intervention, each childbirth event is still closely and cautiously monitored and treated as a potential emergency situation. As mentioned earlier in **D12 (Birth Plan)**, every childbirth is unique and will have its ups and downs, highs and lows. Your birth professional's main job is to do everything necessary to create the greatest possible chances of having a healthy baby and healthy Mama at the end of the day. Your Birth Plan is a guide through the best-case scenario, but you must also be prepared to flex as needed to accommodate the birth professional's best judgement as things develop. Remember the ultimate goal here is healthy Mama and healthy Baby, and your job is not to manage the birth. It is rather to simply do your best to **Be Attentive, Be Calm, Be Competent** throughout the process.

Now that Baby is finally here, let's all pause and reflect for a moment. Mama, Baby, and even you have all worked really hard to get to this point, and now is a good time to enjoy all that you have accomplished. Baby will likely be alert for about an hour or so after the birth, for both bonding with you and Mama and for their first attempt at feeding at the breast. This first hour together is often referred to as "The Golden Hour," and is the perfect time for you to refocus entirely on Mama for a minute and marvel at her power and awesomeness.

Dad Tip #19: Give Mama *all* the love right now. Go out of your way to recognize Mama's experience of her long voyage on this epic journey, starting with "we're pregnant" and ending with just this moment. Specifically, tell her how proud and inspired by her you've been all along the way, and how you've never been happier than just this moment. Tell her how awesome she was throughout the delivery process, and how she is your hero. Tell her how much you appreciated her care and concern for Baby showing up and shining through since Day 1 with her focus on getting the right vitamins, the right food, and the right sleep. Tell her all the things, and most importantly, tell her how much you love her and how you know she is going to be an amazing Mama to your little Baby right there in her arms. *Better connected* indeed!

A great idea is to check in with her preferred Love Languages and consider the option of giving her a pretty necklace or bracelet holding a small charm or pendant with either Baby's name or initial on it. She'll love your thoughtfulness and appreciate your recognition of her journey from Maiden to Mama. Go big here, all the way, she's earned every bit of it.

Chapter 5 Summary for You: This chapter focused on the birth of Baby and specifically focused on how this short time window is where you are really going to be thrust into the spotlight as Mama's trusted partner and accomplice in this whole journey. This period is all about being *better connected* to Mama and her process. We talked about how everything that happens between the first pangs of Labor and you going home with together with Baby is going to be the official **B9 (Birth Story)** and how important your role is in it. This Birth Story is going to be a highlight reel of big moments, so we put a lot of time and energy setting you up for success by giving you specific reminders of how you can *better prepare* to follow **B10 (New Mantra)** of **Be Attentive, Be Calm, Be Competent** all through the process. We covered how Mama's anxiety, and the ensuing adrenaline flood is going to be the biggest impediment to her having a smooth birth. Remember, Oxytocin defeats Adrenaline! So, you getting *better connected* to her may be the biggest factor in getting those anxiety levels down as low as possible so that the Oxytocin can do its job in helping Mama get through the process with the most amount of ease. We also cleared up any misconceptions you might have about Mama's "water breaking" NOT being an emergency in **D16 (Water Breaking)** and reminded you to note the exact time of that event, if it occurs at home, for the birthplace intake questionnaire.

You should have all your *better prepared* ducks in a row at this point, so to speak, with all the various Dad Tips from last chapter covering your Birth Plan, Go Bag, etc.... Therefore, you should be able to spend this time just taking care of Mama and focusing your energy on *better connected* with her and "teaming up" for your upcoming birthing adventure. We talked at length about your role throughout the birth process as being *helpful and supportive* as possible, and included a reminder about how newborns often come out looking exactly as banged up as you might imagine given their recent experience of being born in **D17 (Weird Baby).** At the end of the day, however, it still all boils down to **Be Attentive, Be Calm, Be Competent.**

Once Baby is here out in the world, know how to step right in with a confident "yes!" when asked if you are ready to hold your Baby by going with a side-by-side transfer into the standard **D18 (Cradle Hold)** with Baby's head fully supported and tucked into your left elbow crook and your right arm underneath and across for extra stability. And finally, take this moment to **D19 (Celebrate Mama)** and all her efforts along the way and up through this moment, perhaps adding a small gift into the mix as well. She's been amazing, now is a good time to tell her how much you appreciate it all. Oh yeah, and WELCOME TO FATHERHOOD to you now too!

Chapter 5 Summary for Mama: The onset of sustained and organized contractions marks the last phase of your journey through this pregnancy, and also means that you will finally get to meet and hold your baby soon! This is a super emotional time period for you here Mama, with all the anxiety, excitement, and anticipation swirling and racing through your body at the same time. As much as your man wants to be "in this" with you, he is still fundamentally a separate person from you and your experience "over there," so he needs some help and guidance from you to know where you are and how you are feeling in any given moment. Continue to talk to him and tell him what you are experiencing, and be sure to ask him for specific things when you need his help or support.

Ideally his main role throughout the entire laboring and birth process is to be your rock of physical and emotional support, and to that end I've focused on coaching him up on the mantra of **Be Attentive, Be Calm, Be Competent** throughout each of the stages of childbirth. Just like you though, he's probably never been through this experience before and will be doing the best job he can in any given moment. Feel free to help him help you by requesting specific things or actions when you want them, and be kind and patient with him (as possible, of course) as he struggles to figure things out along the way.

Finally, we covered just the first few minutes or so after Baby is born, and gave him a quick tutorial on how to hold Baby correctly when he first gets the chance. While you've been in Mama-mode since you first discovered that you were pregnant, this moment is a likely a bit of a shock and transition to Dad-mode for him and is a pretty big deal. Give him a hug and squeeze and tell him how happy you are to finally have your new family all together for the first time!

Chapter 6
Welcome to Fatherhood

Baby is finally here!

Wow. You guys did it. You're all 3 cuddled up together, quietly resting together in this first "Golden Hour" right after Baby's birth. Congratulations are in order for each of you, but especially to Mama as this has probably been the most amazing and miraculous ordeal she has ever experienced. This moment is also pretty much when most other "pregnancy guide" type of books end, since, you know, Baby is finally "here" now. However, while your journey *to* the land of Fatherhood is complete, now is when all the real work of being a Dad begins. You didn't think I was just going to walk you to the entrance and then push you through the door while yelling, "Good luck!", did you? While Mama was doing all the work of being pregnant and birthing Baby (with your *help and support*, of course), from here on out you are both going to be fully engaged and involved in your new role as Parents.

As mentioned earlier, this first hour of Parenthood is often referred to as the "Golden Hour" and you'll all 3 most likely be left alone for Baby and Mama to get a full hour of quiet skin-to-skin time. This skin-to-skin time is being increasingly recognized as invaluable for helping Mama and Baby deepen and strengthen their bonds to each other. During this first hour Mama's aforementioned Oxytocin levels are still sky high, and those hormones act almost like a super glue of connecting power for both of them. Often newborns will instinctually seek out and find Mama's breast to try to latch on for their first feeding during this amazing time. It's all pretty amazing stuff!

Regardless of how your particular situation has unfolded, the important thing is that Mama and Baby are both resting comfortably together after this tremendous ordeal they've both just been through, with Mama meeting and holding her long-anticipated Baby, and with Baby snuggling warmly into Mama and being comforted by the familiar sounds of Mama's heartbeat and voice. Many couples report this Golden Hour to be a sacred and profound experience where almost all of the tension and stress of the past 9 months just melts away now that you 3 are finally all together. And many Dads report being blown away by the sight of their brand-new baby, all tiny and helpless, and are moved to tears of joy, relief, and inspiration now that they are finally a "real" Dad. As for skin-to-skin time for Dads and Baby, that's important too! I know how much I enjoyed meeting and snuggling skin-to-skin with my babies shortly after they were born, you should feel free to ask for some skin-to-skin time with your Baby here too.

After that quiet and amazing Golden Hour is over, things may get busy again as the birth attendants return to continue their standard newborn checks and procedures. The weight and length numbers you'll get don't really mean too much, but memorize them anyway because they are pretty much the *only* thing you'll really be asked about for the foreseeable future. It's also standard practice to apply some antibiotic ointment to the baby's eyes, administer a vitamin K shot, and perform a simple heel-prick to get some blood for other various tests. You may have other preferences as spelled out in your Birth Plan so keep that handy to consult with as needed. Most birth facilities will require a 24-hour stay at a minimum, sometimes longer depending on the place's rules for discharge timing. During this 24-hour period the baby will most likely get a hearing test and be closely monitored to make sure the first poop (meconium) has passed. This is an important step in tracking the baby's healthy elimination abilities and overall bodily functions.

For most couples this first 24-hour period is a unique and weird time, perhaps due to the competing urges for excited celebrating and exhausted resting. Celebration because Baby is finally here, yay! Exhausted resting because the emotional rollercoaster of the last 9 months has just concluded with a physically and emotionally demanding experience, and the next chapter of your family journey is already under way. As mentioned earlier, Mama is still all jacked up on Oxytocin, so she'll likely be all smiles and love and light towards you and Baby. Make the most of this and try to simply feel into that love and reflect it back to her. *Better connect* to her here by using lots of your favorite **B6 (Mom Comms)** in line with her favorite Love Languages, especially Physical Touch and Words of Affirmation. Friends and family members will be allowed to briefly visit, and you might find yourself as the Dad having to manage that traffic.

This is also another good time to practice your Red-Yellow-Green light **D14 (Code Words)**. You'll now be able to video chat with your various extended family and friend network as well as start to pack up all your random supplies from your go bags, assuming you've been able to get some sleep and showers by now. Don't forget to give your communications point of contact person the good news to spread, and then let them know you are now good to go on taking back control of things. Most birthing rooms have a Dad cot included, so definitely take a nap if possible after the baby arrives, you'll need your energy back up for what lies ahead! Finally, most birth places will have you read over some educational materials, speak with a lactation consultant, watch a few baby-safety videos, and then sign off on some acknowledgment forms as part of their clearance process.

After you've been cleared for check out, one of the nurses will walk you/wheel Mama out to your car to doublecheck that you have the baby's car seat installed correctly and will then wish you luck and wave goodbye before promptly turning around and walking back into the birthing place. Many, many new Dads I've spoken with tell me that this exact moment often brings the new reality of Fatherhood completely crashing down on top of their heads. "Uh, wait a minute, you're just going to let us drive away now? Don't you know that we have NO IDEA WHAT WE ARE DOING?!" Which brings us right to:

Dad Tip #20: You have NO IDEA what you are doing, and that's 100% OK. That first step off the curb may feel like the biggest single step you've ever taken in your whole life. I think even Neil Armstrong said that this first step into Fatherhood was bigger for him than his first step onto the moon. The ensuing drive home can also feel weirdly surreal for many brand-new Dads. All of the feelings over the previous 9 months of delay and anticipation of "when the baby gets here" were ended when Baby was actually born. Now comes the big bucket of ice water to the face realization of "wow, this is entirely on me to be *this* baby's Dad, not just a "Dad" in the abstract, and this is some seriously important shit!" You may find yourself experiencing a strange combination of joy/dread/shock as you ease the family home in the right lane doing 5 mph under the speed limit for the first time in your life too.

Perhaps you have a trusted friend or relative either with you in the car or waiting at home (one who has hopefully already had a baby or two) to help alleviate some of your first round of worries. But it's OK if you don't, every couple has their own hazing/initiation to go through one way or another. The point is to remember **B2 (Different World)** regarding the evolutionary heritage of delayed Dadness, and that means your feelings of uncertainty, dread, and I'm-in-so-far-over-my-head are all *perfectly normal* and, in fact, actually demonstrate to some degree a very keen awareness of your current situation. A good way to understand this is with my favorite definition of the word "stress" - the potent combination of caring really, really deeply about something while also not having a clear understanding of exactly what you are supposed to do about it all. Sound familiar? If not, ask Mama. ☺

Getting back to arriving home with your new family, you get out of the car, help Mama out of her seat, grab your new baby/baby car carrier, and then dazedly step right into the rest of your life. You're a full-fledged Dad now, 100% legit. Everywhere you go with Baby you are now going to be recognized by other Mamas and Dads as the newest member of the Parent Club. There are no secret handshakes here, just words of congratulations, knowing smiles, and words of encouragement. "Congratulations" will be mixed in with "Enjoy this time while it lasts," interspersed with vague platitudes/warnings of "good luck" and "just you wait." They've all walked this path ahead of you and have had their own experiences of hazing and initiation into the ranks. Hopefully these final few chapters of ***WTF*** make your journey a little easier than was theirs.

Chapter 6 Summary for You: Baby is finally here, whew! Really make it a point to enjoy this next 24-hour period as a sort of "intermission" between the end of the "Pregnancy Journey" and the beginning of the "Parenting Journey." We covered the basics of what most hospitals and birth places will do before sending you, Mama, and Baby back off to your home as a family, and also reminded you of the need to help manage all the visitors and video-chats going on with Mama and Baby. Keep your "Code Words" from **D14 (Code Words)** handy, and use them often! As you head back to your car as a family of three, you'll probably have another moment of shock and confusion when you realize **D20 (No Idea)** and that you are now a full-fledged Dad yet have not a single fucking idea of what you are going to do about it. That's totally expected here, and actually is good evidence of the kind of self-awareness that will serve you well in the coming months. Welcome to Fatherhood!

Chapter 6 Summary for Mama: You are finally holding and snuggling and loving on your brand-new Baby after so many months of waiting and hoping and dreaming. Congratulations Mama, you did it! The birth facility will probably keep you and Baby under observation for at least 24 hours here, please try to use this time to rest up as much as possible. Dad has been coached on what to expect now and on helping you manage all your visitors and video-chats by applying the "Code Words" we covered earlier. Again, help him help you by trying to clearly communicate your wants and needs as regards your energies and interests in engaging with all these friends and family members. You may feel pretty overwhelmed with the whole situation to some degree, but remember, Dad is perhaps feeling this even more intensely. As we said way back at the very beginning of this book, "Women become Mothers when they find out they are pregnant, but Men don't become Fathers until the Baby is born." To whatever degree that is true for you and your man, he may even be almost shell-shocked by this (to him) sudden and severe realization. Be mindful of his experience of all of this, and understand that you both have a lot to learn and a lot of adjusting to do. Heading back home as a new family of three is a huge deal for all of you, and officially marks your new lives as parents. Do your best to try to soak it all in and enjoy this process of discovery together as a team. Congratulations, and good luck!

Chapter 7
The 4th Trimester

Protect & Serve

These first 3 months back at home with a new baby are going to be pretty intense. Fortunately, they are finally starting to be recognized as a distinct time period, almost like a "4th Trimester," that has its own challenges and dynamics for today's parents. Historically speaking, and as covered in **B2 (Different World)**, people used to live with larger family groups with multiple generations and family members all living together under one roof. In those situations, the arrival of a new baby was met with lots of built-in networks of support and help. However, in today's world many new parents come home to empty houses and are far removed from close networks of family and friends to provide the help and support all new parents need.

This new reality around the 4th Trimester time period can be a very difficult one for new parents to transition into with their new roles and responsibilities, especially when parental leave (both maternal and paternal) can vary so drastically from place to place across the country. This leaves us with countless "coming home" scenarios to consider when factoring in the huge range of parental leave possibilities, and a large range of friend and family support possibilities too. The mantra of *better connected, better prepared* has served us well so far, and it still applies going forward here. However, your main challenges as Dad will have shifted, and they all generally fall under the new banner of *Protect & Serve*. Mama, Baby, yourself, and your new family as a whole – Protect & Serve them all.

But before we jump into these challenges, we'll do a quick preview of the typical life flow for the new family, starting with Baby. All the **Big Ideas** and **Dad Tips** in this chapter fall under the Protect & Serve banner, and all of them are deeply interconnected. I'll go over them one at a time and will work them in where I can, but please keep in mind that they all work and flow together. Whichever one I get to last is just as important as whichever one comes up first. You and your family will best be Protected & Served if you start working with all of them from the very first minute you get home with Baby.

New Baby Life

Baby was monitored pretty thoroughly over those first 24 – 48 hours they spent at the birthplace. One of the things that was closely watched was Baby's weight, especially any weight lost since birth. It is very common for babies to steadily lose a little bit of weight over the first few days after birth while their systems (and Mama's) are shifting over from umbilical cord supply of nutrients to a milk/formula supply. Related to this is Baby's ability to process and remove waste and toxins through their kidneys and bowels. To keep an eye on these changes almost all babies go to see their Pediatrician sometime shortly after coming home from the birthplace, usually only 2 or 3 days later. At that visit the Doctor will specifically focus on weight, feeding habits, and number of wet/dirty diapers per day to make sure that the entire digestive system is working properly. There are some great shareable apps out there that make it super easy to keep track of all of these things, such as the one simply named "Baby Tracker." Having a good one is worth the small amount of time it takes to get it downloaded and then up and running. In addition to Baby's weight, they will also get height (length) measurements as well as head circumference measurements. These three measurements of weight, length, and head circumference will be taken at every visit from now on to track the baby's growth and to make sure any hidden health issues are identified as early as possible. These numbers may be the only thing objective you will be able to talk about for the next 6 months and beyond! People will always ask how the new baby is doing, and generally your answer will be something like "well, they are sleeping a lot, and eating, and pooping, but that's about it." Being able to throw in "and they are in the 65% percentile of weight, 70th in height, and 70th in head circumference for their age so things are right on track!" obviously shows you know more about Baby than just poop, so keep these numbers handy. Which brings us right to:

Dad Tip #21: Height, Weight, and Head Circumference are somewhat silly numbers that produce silly conversations. These numbers are the only thing concrete about newborns, so people unfortunately tend to put a strange amount of emphasis on them. The only thing these numbers actually do is help your medical professionals keep track of their *growth over time* so that they can get ahead of any health issues that exist or may develop. For example, imagine a baby born with those numbers all around average (the 50th percentile), but then over time they started to drop down into the 20's relative to age appropriate averages. This drop in percentiles over time tells the Doctor that the baby's rate of growth is mysteriously slowing down. They would then be able to ask more questions and run more tests to try to find out why this is happening. The parents might not have any idea that something might be off. They would still see the baby growing from their outside perspective, but they would not really be able to tell that the baby isn't growing as fast as they should be relative to their age. So, don't put too much emphasis on wherever Baby happens to be on the percentile graphs at any given time and only track how much those numbers go up or down as they get older.

Pro Tip: Babies can bring out all sorts of weird and unhelpful "competitive parenting" instincts in some people, and these can really start to rear their ugly heads in conversations with other parents around the topic of percentages and growth charts. These conversations and comparisons can lead to hurt feelings on everybody's part, leading to all kinds of drama you just don't need to be dealing with right now, if ever. For example, you might have new parent friends that have a big baby that's in the 90's in all of these measurements while your baby might be on the slightly smaller side down in the 40's. Both of these babies are perfectly healthy and happy, one is just bigger than the other for now. Seems simple, right? However, things might start to feel less simple if the other parents seem to gleefully and pridefully talk about how big their baby is, almost as if they are somehow both implicitly claiming that their baby is healthier than yours and also taking credit for/blaming you for the difference in sizes. Again, this is some really weird territory, so try to be sensitive to and aware of this possibility.

In spite of your best efforts, you may or may not find yourself taking these things somewhat personally if these types of comparisons come up, but I guarantee that Mama absolutely is taking them personally. New Mamas are pretty much always close to feeling some sort of anxiety or personal guilt around the question of "Am I being a good Mom?" and can easily take any random Baby-related comment as a direct and personal attack on their Motherhood. These growth chart numbers can be a really big deal for her and can easily lead to lots of weird interactions with other parents of new babies. Watch out for these types of conversations and do your best to try to keep things smooth by working quickly to diffuse any drama you might see brewing around them. If you see or feel a competitive parenting moment coming up, then try to turn the conversation back to how cute the babies are, how cute their outfits are, or spontaneously launch into a funny story about getting baby shit everywhere last time you changed the diaper. Good luck on this one, my friend!

Back to Baby again, there will be additional check-ups scheduled out at 1-week, 2-weeks, 1-month, 2-months, and 4-months and beyond.

These early check-ups will mostly focus on Baby's growth, diaper action, and other basics since the little ones aren't really doing too much else yet. Definitely try to make a note or otherwise keep track of any questions you and Mama might have about the Baby's health and wellness that come up at home in between these check-ups. It's also a good idea to sit down and *better connect* with Mama before Baby's appointment to go over any topics or situations you might want to discuss at the Doctor's office. Those visits can be a bit of a challenge sometimes, especially if Baby is yelling and crying, and it's really easy to forget to ask questions in the middle of all that noise. Having a written note to reference is a good way to *better prepare* you and Mama to both stay focused on the bigger picture and to get the most out of your visit. Please try to make it a priority to go to these check-ups with Mama as a complete family, just simply being present there in the Doctor's office is a great way to Protect & Serve.

Wrapping up Baby's section, while Baby doesn't seem to interact much with the outside world, there is a lot of growth and development going on internally as their brains and bodies adjust to this next chapter of their lives. Keep in mind that they are adjusting to a whole new world, full of new sensory experiences. When they were growing and developing back in Mama's tummy all that time, they never experienced being cold, or being hungry, or even having an experience of pooping. They were always warm and cozy and were never alone, never scared, and never cried. Mama and the umbilical cord took care of everything. Now they are out in the big bright loud world. It can be a bit scary out here! They have small stomachs, and can often be chilly as it takes some time and growth for their brains to get good at regulating their body temperature. They sleep a lot, eat a lot, pee and poop a lot, and can sometimes cry a lot as that is their only way of letting you know that they are cold, wet, hungry, scared or in any way in need of help and attention. They love being warm, being held, and being in close contact with Mama and Dad. That's pretty much it for them. However, like Abraham Lincoln's quote of

"Life isn't so much what happens to you, but how you respond to it that matters," regardless of what they are doing or not doing, how you respond to all that is what really matters here. And that goes for Mama too.

New Mama Life

New Mamas have a lot on their plates here in the US these days. We've talked several times about the disappearing support networks that no longer exist in any meaningful form for many of today's new Mamas. Now we need to bring some other things into the mix that just add so much more uncertainty and worry into the overall new Mama situation. Does Mama have paid maternity leave? For how long? Or not at all? Who is going to watch Baby when she goes back to work? Is she even going to go back to work? What will change at work while she is away? And those questions go on and on. Let's also keep in mind that every other news article is about the dangers of this plastic or that chemical or this birth injury or that kidnapping and countless other monsters and boogeymen lurking around the corner or up on the shelf. And let's not forget all the self-doubt that creeps into many a Mama's head here too. "Am I producing enough milk? Is my baby healthy? Am I a good Mom? How do I avoid making the mistakes my Mom made? How can I be the best Mom possible?" Now throw in sleep deprivation, cracked and bloody nipples, leaky bladders, body image concerns, and you can see how hard it is to be a new Mama.

Unfortunately, the current support systems in play for new Mamas are pretty much just the ones they create themselves from personal and family networks, and thankfully over the internet now too. The only regularly scheduled post-delivery Doctor's appointment focusing on just her health and recovery will be back with her OB at around 6 weeks, and this visit focuses mainly on the medical side of her body recovering and healing from the pregnancy and delivery. There will be a little time devoted to discussing and checking in on her mental and emotional well-being for signs of Post-Partum Depression (PPD), a topic will get into shortly, but for the most part this is an "OK, you're good? Bye." type of visit. In this kind of climate is it any wonder that many women these days are more susceptible than ever to PPD?

This singular and cursory follow-up visit also sharply defines the stark contrast between her new and lonely reality as a Mama versus the abundant amounts of professional help and attention she received when she was a pregnant Mama-to-be. This massive disparity of professional attention and care between before Baby and after Baby leads many new Mamas to justifiably feel like they have been completely abandoned, and right when they are struggling the most and need the most help. You are then left to fill all of those roles and your own brand-new role as a Dad too. Not a good situation for anybody. Which leads us right into our next Dad Tip.

Dad Tip #22: Don't take anything personally. Whatever it is, it probably isn't directly your fault, and it probably isn't your job to fix it. It has been said that new Mamas are living in a state of having almost all their emotions turned up to 10, while also having them all simultaneously jostling about trying to get expressed. If you thought her moods and emotions were already "highly dynamic" during the pregnancy, then buckle your seat belt for the next few months as she tries to get the hang of being a new Mama with all the new demands placed upon her. These varying moods and their dynamic downswings are referred to as "Baby Blues" and can often manifest in sudden and dramatic whirlwinds of emotion. Mama might be feeling great one random afternoon so she decides she's going to wrap up Baby and go for a short walk around the block. 1 minute later you might find her sobbing uncontrollably into the Baby wrap device, crying that she's "a terrible Mom" through the tears, all because she couldn't get the clasp to work properly. I could give you a million examples of these types of rapid cycles, but the point is that in addition to *better* *connecting* with Mama, your role here is to Protect & Serve, and that her emotional well-being is one of the big things that you need to focus on for the next few months. She may on occasion blow up at you or about something you did. Oh, she absolutely will, there is no *may* about it. Fortunately for you, all you really have to do is give her a gentle hug and remind her that you think she's a great Mom, and that Baby is so lucky to have her. Don't worry about trying to use facts and logic here, they don't work. Just gentle hugs and affirmation.

Big Idea # 11: Post-Partum Depression is real, and a real danger to all involved. OK, this is also **Scary Moment #4** that I alluded to earlier, so please take this section to heart. All those stressors I just mentioned above, plus a bunch of other unknowns, can lead to a serious medical condition called Post-Partum Depression (PPD) in some new Mamas, a much deeper and long-lasting change of mood than the highs and lows and ebbs and flows of "Baby Blues." PPD is characterized by a variety of symptoms including disinterest in formerly fun activities, social withdrawal, extreme fatigue and/or anxiety, and certain "non-maternal" feelings towards Baby like resentment, disinterest, or lack of engagement. Look further into PPD on the ***WTF*** website or elsewhere for more details if you're interested, but for our purposes here just know that it can lead to serious consequences for Mama and your family as a whole if left undiagnosed and untreated. In today's society PPD has been estimated to impact up to 20% of new Mamas, and some experts believe it is much more common than that but is underreported due to feelings of shame, embarrassment, and lack of resources.

Unfortunately, many women who start to experience symptoms are also *completely unaware* of their ongoing progression into PPD. That's why it's very important for you to be continuously running your own "independent diagnostic" on her and closely watch her mood and energy levels for at least the first 3 months following Baby's arrival.

Your Pediatrician will run a PPD screen on Mama during every baby check-up by asking a series of questions about her mood, energy, and activities. You must be prepared to interject, or at least have a side conversation with the Doctor, if you think she is actually doing worse on those questions than she is aware of or admits to during the visit. This is no time for holding back your perspective out of concern of not wanting to get her upset or naively hoping that she will somehow just spontaneously get better. YOU are her best defense here, be on point! Protect & Serve! So please stay attuned to how she is doing with everything and seek professional help if it looks like she is starting to show some of these serious symptoms.

An ounce of prevention is worth a pound of cure, and this is especially true for getting ahead of PPD. As our Childbirth Educator, Doula, and friend Allison likes to say, the best prevention for PPD is to simply "Lavish Sisterhood, Limit Stuff."

The Babymoon – Lavish Sisterhood, Limit Stuff

Thinking back to **B2 (Different World)** and times past again, new babies and new Mamas were surrounded by an experienced and friendly community of other Mamas and babies. They had built-in networks of support to provide everything they would need to get off to a great start on their parenting adventure. They got it all – experienced advice, points of comparison, friendly help, shoulders to cry on – everything! This is not the case for many new families now. So, a big part of supporting Mama, and preventing PPD, is to consider looking at this 4th Trimester as "The Babymoon", similar in concept to an extended Honeymoon. It's a special and unique time for Mama and Baby to really just focus on each other, get to know each other and their respective rhythms and rhymes, and not get all caught up just yet in the outside world and its stressors.

Don't worry, this Babymoon cocoon you're helping them build isn't forever, it's just for right now and the next few months. All the extra work you put in now to help Mama and Baby adjust to their new reality and strengthen their bonds will create a firm and strong foundation for building a better future for all of you together. During this Babymoon it's really important for you to Protect & Serve by doing your part to help accommodate the Lavish Sisterhood, Limit Stuff directive. Let's start with the "Sisterhood" bit:

1) As mentioned before, you probably have a new batch of new friends you gathered throughout the pregnancy that now also have new babies. Try to make an effort to set up "baby dates" with these new friends, either at one of one of your houses or at a park/playground. Pro Tip – restaurants are terrible places to have a baby date. You want someplace that is relaxing for Mama if and when Baby cries or needs to nurse. Then, during the baby date, grab your counterpart Dad (and maybe the babies too) and give the new Mamas some leisurely time to chat and hangout together, one-on-one. Taking the babies with you isn't too important though, the main point is to give the Mamas a chance to just connect with each other and talk about their new Mama experiences without you guys being around as part of the audience.
2) Encourage Mama to invite important people in her life to come in to town for a short visit, regardless of how you feel about them. Choose guests who can be helpful "villagers" and not just "Baby tourists." The kind of guests who will easily pitch in around the house and who understand what Mama is going through right now. Remember, your job is to Protect & Serve now, and playing extra nice with her sister or Mom or annoying college roommate is a small burden you can bear here. Bonus points if you reach out to them yourself and suggest a visit! Regardless, for any out-of-towners, the visit

should be just for 3 days or so, an optimum amount of time to be helpful and enjoyable without drifting into annoying.

3) Suggest (and initiate) frequent FaceTime or video chats with extended family and friends who don't live nearby. It's actually probably more helpful for her to have daily check-ins with friends and family than it would be to be overwhelmed with a constantly revolving door of house guests all coming and going one after another. Today's technology makes that easier than ever, and you might be surprised at how powerful a 5-minute video chat can be for lifting Mama's spirits.
4) Suggest that she reconnect with her existing friends and their previously enjoyed group activities such as yoga, brunch, or whatever while you plan to take Baby out on an adventure to get groceries or something, or even just a nice walk in the woods or park. Huge Dad Card credits here! She'll absolutely miss Baby though, even if they are only apart for 45 minutes, so send her some frequent pics of you two having fun while you are out and about, and absolutely ZERO pics of the baby crying. That way she'll be able to relax into her activity a bit more and enjoy her friends and their company. Bonus Man Card points for a pic of you wearing a sleeping Baby. Win, win - *$Ka-ching$!*

"Limiting Stuff" can be a little bit trickier than "Lavishing Sisterhood" for many reasons, not the least of which is the fact that our current culture is absolutely swimming in "stuff." Look at your Baby Registry and see how much "stuff" is in there. Look at the nursery with all its themes and colors and mobiles and lights and sounds. So much stuff! Here's the deal though. Babies only need a few simple things. They want to be held. A lot. Pretty much all the time, and that's OK. They want to eat, preferably breastmilk. And often, and that's OK too. They like to sleep a lot (thank goodness!!), and don't like a wet bottom (who does?). So that is what Mama's job (and yours) boils down to right now, just to take care of those few essential things. Everything else is just "stuff." Babies don't care about toys, giraffes on the wall, or if the crib collapses into a bassinet or not, so adjust your priorities and expectations accordingly. Here are some simple suggestions to Protect & Serve when it comes to "Limiting Stuff" for these first 3 months:

1) Don't get too aggressive in scheduling activities on weekends or evenings. Sure, you want to go out and live your lives and have fun and show off your new baby. But both Mama and Baby need a lot of downtime and rest. So just remember that element and try to take it easy, at least for the next few months. Activities are "Stuff" too.
2) While they are a crucial part of the "Lavish Sisterhood" directive, remember that social visits also fall into the category of "stuff" to be limited. Request all interested visitors call or text ahead to check to see if the timing of a visit will work out. Remind Mama about the **D14 (Code Words)** and request that she use them frequently to help keep you in the loop as her energy levels change. A social visit that ends too soon is easier to work with than one that goes on too long. And it is totally your job here in Protect & Serve mode to speak up when it's time to end the visit. A simple, "Hey, we really appreciate you coming by to visit, but Mama and Baby didn't sleep well last night and its almost nap time. Thanks again for swinging by, we look forward to seeing you again soon" will usually get them up and out pretty quickly if you get the Red Light "Tomato" Code Word from Mama.
3) All the gifts, presents, and things you bought for Baby really don't need to be opened, sorted, put away, and/or posted up on social media right away. There is plenty of time for that later. Sure, if Mama is feeling good and is well rested and wants to jump right in, then great, go for it. But remind her to set small goals and do your part to put things in closets at least so she doesn't have piles of "stuff" sitting around silently

judging her. Pick and choose your times wisely if you are looking to clear up your Gift Tracker Spreadsheet from **D9 (Gift Tracker),** otherwise all those gifts can wait until later.

4) Baby announcements, "Thank You" cards, and all that other social expectation "stuff" can also wait. Many Mamas who are heading back to work, whether in 3 weeks or 3 months, feel like the Maternity Leave window is when they are "supposed" to do all the things that they feel they need to do. They put lots of pressure on themselves to "get it done while they can," but this pressure is absolutely not needed now. If you and Mama have the time and energy to work on these things here and there, then great. But if she appears to be overly stressing about it then you should absolutely feel free to either offer to help get ahead on those things (even if you don't want to), or remind her that there will be plenty of time later when her energy is back up to get to them. In any event, anything "stuff-related" that makes this time harder for Mama should be limited as much as possible.

As we've discussed above, this 4th Trimester is a time of big transitions and adjustments for everybody. The bonds and relationships that all 3 of you form now are a big part of the foundation for supporting the new family challenges that follow. And while it may occasionally seem interminable, this short window of time will indeed go by quickly and will soon come to an end. Remember, it's not forever, it's just for right now. Ideally, as this time goes by Mama and Baby (and you) will start to develop some shared rhythms and rhymes and will begin to establish some healthy routines that work best for the whole family. From the *better prepared* angle, questions that should be answered during this time include Baby's sleeping arrangement, rough routines around feeding, sleeping, and diaper-changing schedules, stroller, car seat, and baby wearing device workings and transfers, and other general daily routines that are going to need to be communicated to any other child care helpers.

There are plenty of resources out there to help Mamas get through this initial time in the healthiest ways possible, but you are her main support. Protect & Serve!

New Dad Life

Ideally you got ***WTF*** early enough in your pregnancy, read it, and were then able to start to implement some of the ideas and suggestions in here as the pregnancy progressed along. Hopefully you were therefore able to get to this point of the journey with your head mostly above water, rather than perhaps buried someplace else, and now have your eyes locked onto the distant shore. You've done the basic prep work of getting *better connected* to Mama and *better prepared* for Baby, so now it's time to step it up further into to the next level of the Dad Zone.

But even if you just picked up ***WTF*** for the first time, and/or hung out way to long in the Dud Zones, that's OK too. Everything that came before Baby's arrival is just like a few small appetizers you snack on until the rest of the dinner suddenly shows up at your table all at once. You had a few chicken wings or maybe a bite of the spinach dip along the way to whet your appetite, but now the 20oz Ribeye is hitting the table, and so are the garlic mashed potatoes and creamed spinach. And oh yeah, if that wasn't enough, Mama and Baby over at the other table just sent you 3 more side dishes, a lobster tail, and another cocktail. Hope you're hungry!

Big Idea #12: Own your role as Dad, and *everything* that comes with it. Many guys struggle mightily with the job of Dad, and a large percentage of that struggle comes from them fighting against their new reality and its responsibilities, either consciously or unconsciously. If you go all-in 100% for these first 3 months that make up the 4th Trimester then you will be in the best position possible to make smart and timely as-needed adjustments later. The more you try to preserve "the way things were," the more it's all going to work out poorly for everybody – Mama, Baby, and you. Remember, it's all about Protect & Serve right now.

Here's an easy example of what that might look like. Paul has a group of buddies that he plays golf with every week, they even have a standing 11am tee time reserved on Saturdays at their favorite course. They go at 11am because that gives them some time at home in the mornings with their families before they head off for a long day away at the golf course. Most outings end with a beverage and snack back at the clubhouse, and then they all head back to their homes in time for dinner. All together Paul is usually gone from around 10am – 5pm or so. And that's great, it works for everybody involved. At least it did. But now Paul and his wife just welcomed a new baby into their lives. If Paul is smart and accepts his role as Dad, he will tell his buddies – "Hey, I'm taking some time off from our golf outings. We just had the baby and I don't want to make any commitments to you guys about golfing for the foreseeable future. My focus and priority are to take care of my new family. Once all of that settles into a workable routine where golfing isn't such a challenge then I'll circle back to you guys. In the meantime, feel free to find a replacement for me, have fun, and hit 'em straight!" All good here! Paul was clear with himself so he was then easily able to be clear with his buddies. Dad Card credits for taking care of his family first, and Man Card credits for speaking frankly to his buddies about it. Win, win, *$ka-ching$!*

However, if Paul was not owning his role 100% for now and was trying to quickly get back to "the way things were" then he might say something like "Hey guys, I'm going to have to skip this week since we just brought the baby home but definitely count me in for next week." He would then find himself feeling "stuck" when the next week rolled around and he was trying to get out the door to go have fun with his golf buddies while Mama was on the couch and had gotten no real sleep in two weeks and was holding crying Baby and asking him what time he was going to be back. Paul is now facing a lose-lose situation where he loses connection to his family if he heads out to the golf course, and he loses the respect of his buddies if he decides to suddenly cancel at the last minute. Holding on to "the way things were" when they aren't anywhere near that way now is a great way to experience lots of these "forced-loss" moments. Is getting back to having fun with your golf buddies more important than being present to Protect & Serve Mama and Baby right now? I hope not.

I'm now going to get into one of the biggest new Dad challenges that many guys face, and one that I have received the most questions about over these past few years – the immense power of a crying baby. I can relate to these concerns directly on a personal level as well, for two reasons. The first is that our second baby had bouts of colic on and off for several months after she was born. Colic is not really an official medical diagnosis, it is just a fancy word for when Baby cries inconsolably for long periods at a time, and these episodes often occur daily and stretch out over the course of several months. This is a temporary condition with no certain causes or cures, and usually fades away as mysteriously as it comes on. However, the lived experience of having a colicky baby at home is very hard for everybody, and I can personally attest to it being very hard for me and my wife too. The second and much more impactful reason is that a former co-worker of mine had his life completely destroyed when an overwhelmed family member succumbed to the power of a crying baby and lashed out angrily at his baby. He and his whole family suffered immensely as a result, so I'll get right into that situation here next.

Big Idea #13: The power of a crying baby, Part 1. This is the **5th** and final **Scary Moment** where I'm going to grip you tightest by your shirt collar and "get real" with you for a minute. This is also perhaps the scariest of the Scary Moments too. Before you left the hospital or birthplace you probably watched a few educational videos on your new baby and its needs, and one of them probably talked about Shaken Baby Syndrome (SBS). You might have been horrified by the reality that SBS even exists, and rightly so. SBS can cause *permanent and catastrophic* damage to the baby's brain, many of whom then grow up requiring constant and fulltime medical care for the rest of their lives. SBS is not at all fixable, but is 100% avoidable. What leads to SBS almost 100% of the time is the baby crying inconsolably, and many of the people that end up violently shaking a screaming baby are men. That's you here, Dad. Why is this the case?

Generally speaking, the sound of a crying baby provokes strong reactions in all people, even more so if the crying continues to go on for more than a few minutes. For new Mamas this strong reaction is usually an instant and overwhelming spike of anxiety in her brain (and rightly so, evolutionarily speaking). Mama will usually rush right over to Baby when they're crying, scoop them up into her arms, and immediately start swaying and shushing and cooing to Baby. If none of her attempts to sooth Baby seem to work and the crying persists, then many Mamas get overwhelmed with the massive amounts of anxiety and frustration and can burst into tears, sobbing "I don't know what's wrong, I don't know what to do!!" as they try all the various measures they can think of to sooth the baby.

Many men, on the other hand, have a very different visceral reaction to prolonged exposure to a crying baby – one of extreme anger and rage. Rather than having anxiety as the main emotion welling up in them, threatening to short circuit the system into a tear-filled breakdown, many men report feelings of anger and rage surging through their bodies as Baby continues to cry in spite of their efforts to sooth them. If this emotional cascade spirals out of control then anger can explode into an act of aggression for a man, even grabbing the baby and viciously shaking it back and forth, while screaming

"STOP CRYING!" at the top of his lungs. **THIS IS ALL BAD**. And this is what happened to my co-worker's baby. Even one or two seconds of violent shaking will cause serious brain damage in Baby. *Permanent and catastrophic* brain damage. If this happens to you then your whole world will collapse in on you and will absolutely crush you. Your baby will go to the hospital, you will go to jail, and Mama and everybody else will hate you *forever*. **No fucking joke here.** So, be *highly vigilant* of yourself when Baby's crying starts to wear on you, and even more so if they keep crying in the face of your best efforts to soothe them. If you feel too much angry energy rising up, do not let it explode into aggression. This isn't a stub-your-toe-so-smash-the-coffee-table moment. Simply recognize you may be nearing your Tilt Zone, gently lay screaming Baby down someplace safe, and just walk away for a few minutes. Go out in the garage and shout at the wall, or go hit the punching bag 10 times, or 100. Do something, anything, but **never ever, ever, ever shake your Baby**. Ever. Enough said.

The power of a crying baby, part 2. Wow, Part 1 above was intense! Whew, let's take a deep breath or two here and get back to the Protect & Serve framework. As I mentioned above, Mamas are programmed to pretty much immediately react to the sound of crying by rushing over and attending to Baby. This mechanism essentially cuts off all abstract thinking for a moment, correctly allowing her to focus all of her attention on the here and now of Baby and their needs. Most of the time Baby will be crying because they are hungry, or wet, and/or want to snuggle with Mama. After all, physical security is Nature's highest priority. So, most of the time Mamas will scoop up baby, quickly check their diaper, and then sit down to cuddle and nurse Baby on the comfy couch or chair.

After about 1 minute of getting Baby settled down the big impulse of anxiety from just a moment ago melts away into the potent cocktail of love and relaxation that comes with the cascade of hormones released while breastfeeding. Remember, our friend Oxytocin from childbirth is also released during breastfeeding and is a powerful antidote to anxiety. And almost like clockwork, two other things are likely to happen. First, she will slowly "come back" to whatever was happening right before Baby started crying – "sorry babe, what were we talking about?" Second, she will start looking around for something to drink because nursing Baby always makes Mama *immediately* thirsty. The problem may then may arise that her cup or bottle of water is upstairs or wherever else she last left it, so she will then look over at you and ask you to grab her some water. This will happen a lot. She will *always* go to the baby right away when she hears them crying, and will *never* stop and think "oh, wait, where's my water, I should bring it with me because I will be thirsty when I sit down to nurse Baby." Therefore, if you are smart, you will strategically place lots of bottles of water all over the house, concentrating them in known nursing spots like the rocker, the couch, wherever. Every time she sits down to nurse, then gets thirsty, then realizes she left her water back in the bathroom, then remembers you have set her up with a stash where she can reach it, she will pause and internally thank you for being such a great Dad, teammate, and partner. Win, win, *$Ka-ching$*

Dad Tip #23: Use your Dad tools to conquer the crying. Remember those headphones from **D10 (Top 10)** gifts for new Dads? Those are for you, and for exactly those situations when Baby seems determined to cry it out for a while in spite of your best efforts to feed, change, cuddle, and comfort them. Even a simple cheap pair of work site type headphones or ear plugs will work wonders here. Obviously better are the Bluetooth audio kind where you can put on some soothing music for yourself, or even a podcast if you're up for that. The main point is that muffling the sound of Baby crying, even just a little bit, takes almost all of the tilt-inducing power away from it by blunting both the sharpness and the volume.

While it still sucks 100% when Baby is having a meltdown, at least with headphones on you can still remain both physically and emotionally present for Baby while they scream away in your arms. You will still be trying to gently rock and sway and shush and smile and pat and do all the right things to try to help and sooth Baby, but you will be doing so with a smile on your face rather than going beet-red as you try to choke down the rising fury and anger. Remember, Baby is obviously having some sort of terrible internal experience right now, and you are indeed helping just by being physically and emotionally present. Important caveat here – the headphones are absolutely NOT to be used to help you *ignore* your Baby, they are to be used as a tool to help you better *attend* to your Baby. This is a very important distinction, especially from Mama's point of view.

Remember "The Shusher" from our **D10 (Top 10)** list too? That is another perfect helping tool for when Baby is crying inconsolably. Just try making a prolonged "shushing" sound with your mouth for 30 seconds. Now try it for 3 minutes. 10 minutes? Impossible. Now you're completely out of breath and Baby is still crying. Bring in The Shusher! This device saved my sanity many times - at 2 in the morning, on long car drives, and everywhere in between. It has a 15-min or 30-min timed setting and variable volume control. The sound of Mama's heartbeat in the womb is surprisingly loud, so The Shusher can be used at a pretty decent volume to help Baby find an internal comfort space. In any event, most crying babies love the sound of The Shusher, and it can provide a much steadier stream of sound than you over there huffing and puffing away ever could.

Aside from the assist provided from the above items, the most effective strategies for helping to sooth a crying baby are known as the "5 S's." As covered by Dr. Harvey Karp in his book The Happiest Baby on the Block, the 5 S's are Swaddle, Side or Stomach position, Shush, Swing, and Suck.

1. Swaddle – Babies love being swaddled up nice and snug. This helps them relax and limits the startle reflex while also recreating the safe confines of the womb.
2. Side or Stomach position – Current sleeping protocols for babies recommend back only, but side or stomach position when holding is much more effective at calming Baby down.
3. Shush – Again, recreating the womb sounds helps calm baby down. There are even special soundtracks available that are engineered to more closely replicate those specific sounds.
4. Swing – The womb is an active environment, and babies seem to get calmer the more active it is. Think about our pregnant zebra getting away from the lions from earlier. Quick little bounces will help Baby chill out faster than slow rhythmic swinging.
5. Suck – On the boob, a pacifier, or even a (clean) finger-tip in an emergency, engaging the sucking reflex also helps calm Baby down.

I won't get further into those here, but they are time tested techniques for helping calm Baby that largely imitate the comfort of the womb environment. Please look into this further on your own or in the reference section of the ***WTF*** website if you like. There are also tons of simple demonstration type videos online for you and Mama to look through together to earn a few more *better connected* Dad Card credits.

Baby crying is a huge thing, and a huge worry for most new parents, so we jumped right in and covered that first. Almost the entire rest of this chapter will consist of specific Protect & Serve **Dad Tips** that come from the previously framed **B12 (Own It All)** of fully embracing your role as Dad now. Whenever you are feeling stuck or frustrated or all jammed up about what's going on in front of you with Mama and/or Baby, just put the following questions to yourself: "What does fully stepping into the role of Dad look like *right here*? What does my family need from me *right now*? What *specific thing* can I do to help everybody out in the bigger picture *right now*?" My Air Force buddy Kirby likes acronyms, so he goes with WIN: What's Important Now? Answers to these questions will keep you out of the Dud Zones and help move you further into the Dad Zone. Whatever works for you, find a way to help you connect to the bigger picture where the answer relates to Protect & Serve. These next **Dad Tips** give you some specific strategies to make that whole process easier for everybody. For at least this 4th Trimester time period anyway. You can renegotiate as needed later on.

Dad Tip #24: Just do it. Everything. Changing diapers, feeding Baby, cooking, cleaning, Baby baths, everything. Just do it all. Don't wait to be asked, don't pretend not to see what needs to be done, don't think anything at all is "not your job." Don't Dud Zone on these things, go Dad Zone all the way right now. For these first 3 months home as a new family, do everything. You and Mama can figure out your individual longer-term preferences and routines in more detail later on after things settle down a little bit. But for now, just do everything. I've heard some guys inexplicably say things like "Real Men don't change diapers!" and to them I've said "What? You're scared of a little bit of shit on your hands?? How *manly*... Now stop whining and take care of your damn kid!" You will gain huge Man Card credits by being able to competently look after your newborn in all areas rather than just standing there helplessly in the door while Mama runs in to take care of things. You will also gain huge Dad Card credits when Mama is happily telling her friends how you are being so awesome and fully jumping into your new Dad role, especially when she hears some of her friends complaining about how their husbands can't even look at a diaper and ran off golfing and drinking with their friends again last Saturday. Win, win, *$ka-ching$*

Dad Tip #25: New Dad Blues Busters. We introduced the phrase "Baby Blues" earlier when discussing New Mama Life and its emotional challenges, so let's now shift over to our version - the New Dad Blues - and drill down into that a deeper. Most Dads in the US today work some kind of job out of the house, and also get little or no paid time off for Paternity Leave. So, after a week or so home with Mama and Baby, most Dads are headed back out to their job situation and its regular routines. Not ideal, and not what a lot of other countries do, but it is what it is (for now). How is a new Dad supposed to feel anything but beat up and downtrodden if his life is one big carousel of obligations and sucking it up and putting everybody and everything else first? If you aren't careful, and are under-rested, underfed, and underappreciated, then the New Dad Blues can seep right into your life. Not good for you, not good for being able to Protect & Serve your family either. The following items are some specific things that you can do to head off the New Dad Blues and to make that back-to-work transition easier for yourself and for your family:

1) **Food**. Remember that crock-pot/pressure cooker from the Top 10 list? Now is when it comes in handy. Before you head off to work, simply throw some chicken, rice, and the sauce or dressing of your choice into the cooker. Set the timer so that it's all finished cooking around 5pm or whenever you normally eat dinner. The beauty of these types of dishes is once they are done cooking, they then stay hot and ready in the crockpot until whenever you are ready to sit down and eat them. They also only involve minimum clean-up efforts when finished. Easy-Peezy. Boom. Done. Healthy dinner for your family, all set up and ready to go whenever you are. Dad Card credits, *$ka-ching$!*

2) **Decompress**. Before you had the drama of a brand-new family waiting for you back at the house you might have come straight home from work after a long day, looking forward to just chilling out with a beer and sitting on the couch for 20

minutes while you mentally and emotionally decompressed. That shit won't fly anymore Dad, there are new rules in play. You need to take your mental break before you even pull in the driveway now. I've had some Dads tell me that they stop just around the corner and sit in their car for 15 minutes before pulling in the driveway. Others take their mental break in the workplace parking lot before heading home. I'd recommend something halfway in between whereby you've clearly "left work" and equally clearly haven't "gotten home" quite yet. Preferably a park or something with a pretty view of the water, an open green space, or even just some trees and flowers. 15 minutes somewhere between work and home to intentionally clear your mind of work drama and reconnect to your role of Dad – to Protect & Serve your family. When your 15-minute transition is over you can then ease on home, ready to tag in on Baby right away.

3) **Tag in**. Prepare to tag in on Baby the minute you walk in the door, or at least have that as your mentality. Maybe give Mama a quick smooch and let her decompress for a few minutes first, but then just sweetly tell her to go take some time to herself while you take care of Baby. Ideally you pack up the little bambino and go for a short walk around the block, or even just out to the garage or back yard for a spell. Obviously don't push to head out right away if both Mama and Baby are well rested and happy to see you, don't wake Baby up if they are sleeping, and don't interrupt them if they are nursing. The larger point is that you should expect to "clock-in" as Dad the second you walk through the door, and often the best way to clearly show Mama (and Baby) that you are doing this is to fully take over Baby management and give Mama a chance to take a shower, write some emails, go to the bathroom, or whatever else she hasn't been able to get to yet

because she's been managing the Baby all by herself for the entire day.

4) **You time**. Manage your personal time accordingly. You will obviously need to back-burner any number of your usual Dude Zone hobbies and interests for a little while, especially the more time-consuming ones like golf, binge-watching TV, or using your season tickets to your local sports team. However, to keep the New Dad Blues at bay you still need to make some time just for yourself to recharge your batteries and refresh your outlook. Your lunchbreak at work is the easiest time to do this now, but you can also try to take some time early in the morning before work or later in the evening after Mama and Baby have first gone down to sleep (this will be early). Whether your thing is going for a run, sitting in meditation, or reading up on Roman History, make sure to make at least a little dedicated time throughout the week for it and for yourself. The point here is that you *intentionally* make time to do what you need to do to take care of yourself and charge up your Man Card credits, but do so in a way that does not take time away from your Dad duties.

5) **Us time.** Mama may not be as interested in your work life, nor as good a conversationalist in general as she used to be, at least for a while. Hopefully you and Mama have a good foundation of open communication as a part of your relationship. One where she is aware of what is going for you at work, is interested in those changing circumstances, and understands that it is important for you to be able to speak with her about them. However, as a new Mama her brain is working very differently now. Baby and its life and needs are priorities #1, 2, and 3 for her right now, and the better you understand that and tailor your approach to communication differently, the better off all 3 of you will be.

Here's an easy example of what that looks like in practice. Say you had a great day at work and really hit a home run with a presentation to your boss or an important client. Awesome, well done, Sir! You are rightfully excited about this and want to share your story with Mama when you get a chance. So, after crushing it with tagging in on Baby for the first 30 min you are home, you then sit down to the dinner that's happily and easily waiting for you in the crockpot. So far, so good. You get three bites in and Mama says "How was work today, babe?" You excitedly start to tell her your story and then hear a slight whimper from the rocker next to the table and see Baby's hand move a little. No big deal, right? You just keep on rolling in your story, barely missing a beat. Not Mama!

That whimper you just heard started a hormone cascade in her brain and now your story is starting to sound a lot like Charlie Brown's teacher "whaa whaa wha-whaa." Her attention is pulled to Baby, who then makes another whimper and starts to cry. Mama suddenly stands up, gets Baby out of the rocker, and then starts to nurse Baby, sitting back down at the table and, after getting settled back in, says "Sorry babe, you were telling me about that client?" She was genuinely interested in hearing it, but Baby's crying triggered the "Baby button" and she instantly and automatically tuned you out while she was getting Baby up and latched on to the boob. But now she's back, right? Wrong. You start back in on your story and 15 seconds later look over to see her gazing lovingly down at Baby, totally not paying any attention to you and your story. You are now seeing Oxytocin, the "love hormone" we talked about earlier that helped Baby come out, back in action. It kicks in during breastfeeding, transporting Mama away to that loving place of the warm and squishies for her darling little bundle of joy.

Your "important presentation" just can't compare, sorry Dad, nothing personal. But that's OK, because you now know how this whole Dad life works. So, keep your work stories short and to the point. Focus on feeling-descriptions (It felt great!) rather than going deep into the play-by-play. And remember, while it may seem that when Baby is happily nursing is a great time to get into the story, that's just not at all the case. When you see Mama and Baby happily nursing you are better served, as is your family, by you switching gears and simply saying "You are such a great Mama, I can feel your love for Baby from way over here, I'm so happy with our new little family." Win-win, *$ka-ching$!*

6) **Shift sleep.** This final part of this "Back to Work" section is pretty crucial to your whole family's success, and that involves everybody getting something resembling a decent night's rest. A good night's sleep may in fact be your best overall antidote to the New Dad Blues. The over-tired new parents are a solid stereotype, based in the hard reality that babies don't sleep for long periods of time and they do cry for help and attention pretty often, especially upon waking up. The fundamental mistake that many new parents make here is that they struggle to the precise degree that they try to make Baby fit into their old life and its routines. They often have Baby in their own separate room while they both try to go to bed together in theirs, falsely imagining that this is going to do anything but make all 3 of them miserable. Baby will usually wake up repeatedly throughout the night, hungry and/or wet and/or scared, and will start crying. That's what babies are supposed to do. That crying will wake both of you up, and you will be figuring out how to make Baby happy and/or how to go back to sleep before Baby does this again in 2 hours. Not good. The solution? Shift Sleeping!

I'll tell you how that worked for us, but obviously feel free to improvise things to fit your lifestyles and schedules accordingly. Shortly after coming home with our first baby we decided to try out Shift Sleeping. My lovely wife Jenn is naturally a more early-to-bed type and I'm more naturally a night owl, so the question of how to break up the shifts was pretty straightforward for us. She would go to bed by herself upstairs at 8pm or so, and set her alarm to go off at 2am. I would stay downstairs awake and/or resting/sleeping on the couch while snuggling with Baby or laying him in the bassinet next to me. I was right there for him the whole time, and was quick to change a diaper, give him a bottle (my wife pumped extra breastmilk throughout the day, but formula is cool too), and attend to all his needs. My wife would be upstairs getting 6 straight hours of uninterrupted sleep, helped along by her own white noise machine on the bedside table blocking any of Baby's random cries echoing up from downstairs. Around 2am her alarm would go off and she would come sleepily trudging down the stairs while I dragged myself up them, briefly exchanging a "status report" on Baby in passing. I would then set my alarm to go off at 8am and also get around 6 straight hours of pure, clean sleep while she napped on the couch and hung out with Baby downstairs. Although it took some time to get used to, this Shift Sleeping arrangement worked out perfectly for us. We both got a decent chunk of straight sleep every night, and often got an extra hour or three of napping while "on-duty" too. Baby had one of us right there all night next to him and was able to be cuddled and snuggled and held almost immediately at all times. Win for everybody!

Dad Tip #26: Protect & Serve, but only up to a point. Something you might have noticed happening to you the minute that you first saw brand new Baby in your arms is what I call the activation of "Dad

Brain." Different from the delayed Dad Instinct covered in **B2 (Different World),** Dad Brain is what tells you that you have much bigger priorities to deal with now so you better tighten up the ship at work, with your finances, and anywhere else you might have been coasting mindlessly along while back in the Dude Zone. And this activation is a good thing! But Dad Brain also can get you wound up a little tighter than necessary sometimes, especially if you are still feeling a bit of life shock from the whole transition and are also a bit under-rested as well. This can manifest as a strange over-aggressive vigilance when you are in Protect & Serve mode, so you need to keep an eye on how that energy is coming up so that you don't get yourself in trouble over minor trifles. Here are a couple of examples from my experience with this for you to laugh at:

1) I was leaving a grocery store and had Baby with me in the shopping cart. As I approached the crosswalk, I saw a car slowly coming from the right about 20 feet away or so. I started to step into the crosswalk since we had the right-of-way and there was a stop sign for the car, but the car suddenly sped up to cross in front of us. It was at least 15 feet away at its closest point, and never in danger of actually hitting us, but my Protect & Serve energy shot through the roof and I had to rein in the urges to run after the car and get the person that "almost hit my kid." I was totally happy and calm one second, and then absolutely infuriated and pulsing with rage the next. Whoa!

2) One evening we were out having dinner at a casual sidewalk café and Jenn started breastfeeding Justin at the table while we waited for our food to arrive. I noticed an older lady sitting a few tables away looking at them and whispering to the other old ladies at her table. She did this a few times, obviously talking about my wife nursing in public. I could feel the Protect & Serve energy coming on-line and was trying to figure out

how to address this lady if she decided to step to my wife to chastise her about nursing in public. Guess what happened next? That old lady looks over one more time, stands up, and starts to walk over to our table. I'm seriously trying to remind myself that, no matter what, I absolutely cannot punch this old lady's head clean off her shoulders. As I brace myself and squeeze the chair under my legs she quickly leans over and says to Jenn, "I just want to thank you for having the courage to feed your baby in public. You are an amazing Mom and are showing other Moms that it's OK to feed their baby whenever they are hungry, wherever you may be. Good job and God bless you!" She smiled broadly and went back to her table of other ladies, all of whom were now smiling too. Silly me. I was ready to go to war with an old lady who was merely coming over to congratulate us.

This Protect & Serve energy's ability to go from 0 - 100 in a flash is a necessary relic of evolution. Back in the day, if a bear jumped out at your family in the woods then your body and brain needed to be hardwired and primed for instant and aggressive Protect & Serve action. And that flash activation still has some small degree of relevance for today's world too. However, the trick is to be aware of this primal urge and understand that you need to actively dial it back in 99.9% of the circumstances you'll face. Regardless of what Granny had to say to my nursing wife above, murderous rage would have been a terrible way to respond. So, check yourself with the Protect & Serve stuff, especially with old ladies.

Dad Tip # 27: Fathers don't Mother. This is a big one, and definitely make sure Mama reads this one. Twice. I'll even say it again - *Fathers don't Mother*. What I mean by this is that you absolutely do NOT need to do everything the exact same way that Mama does it. In fact, unless it is an actual safety issue, like securing Baby in the car seat straps correctly, then you should feel free to do pretty much anything "your way" rather than getting into silly conversations and arguments about who's "doing it right." For a quick example of what I mean, right now just cross your arms in front of your chest the way you normally would do it. OK, now intentionally cross them the other way. If you are a right-over-left kind of guy, then try going left-over-right, and vice versa. Have Mama try this too. Feels weird as shit when you do it "wrong", right? Like, what normal person could possible cross them this "other" way? As a matter of fact, people are pretty evenly divided between right-over-lefters and left-over-righters. Who knew?

This example is a great metaphor for about a million and one issues when it comes to taking care of all things Baby, and pretty much everything else around the house too. Maybe you are a handle-up silverware washer and she is handle-down, or you are a football-hold-the-baby and she is a cradle-hold-the-baby kind of person. Whatever it is, just don't worry about which way is "right," and don't pester the other person about "doing it wrong" unless it is a legitimate safety issue. Most of these things will naturally drift to a single way of doing them, but don't feel like you need to park in one of the Dud Zones about it and either put your foot down and have an argument or just defeatedly do it the "way she tells you."

Dad Tip #28: Dad Zone Maintenance and Upkeep. Just because you are now a Dad doesn't mean that you've permanently placed yourself in the Dad Zone. Let's face it, we all know that guy that just pulled into Wimpytown somewhere along the way and put the car in park. He may have been making his way slowly towards the Dad Zone, but then just gave up on the struggle and turned into a defeated and downtrodden "Yes, dear..." Wimpytown Dad after Baby arrives. He got so used being *helpful and supportive* by catering to his lady's every want and need when she was pregnant (as did she), that he never successfully stepped back out into the world as his own independent person. Man Card, revoked.

We also probably know that guy over in the other Dud Zone of Jerkville who hasn't quite seemed to have gotten the memo about the Dad Zone and taking his Dad role more seriously. He's still going out to the bar on Friday nights with his buddies and doing whatever else he likes while his lady is at home by herself (again) with their new baby. "I'm not the one nursing the baby, you are!" Dad Card, fail. Both these guys have missed the big picture, and good arguments can be had about which one of these Dud Zone "misses" is the bigger fool. The way to avoid these two Dud Zones is to think about how to work with your new situation and strive to find ways through it that allow you to have both your Man and Dad cards in your wallet, and both loaded full of credits. *$ka-ching$*. The two most important things that will help you succeed here are strategic communication and strategic planning, as follows below.

1) **B6 (Mom Comms)** reloaded. Think back to our earlier discussions in **B6 (Mom Comms)** and **B8 (Teamwork)**. Those same lessons apply here in the Dad Zone too. Look for opportunities to fill up Mama's bank with Love Language credits. You'll be doing lots of "extra things" now anyway, so you might as well be smart about it and focus on *specific* things, words, and actions that get you the most bang for your buck. On the flip side, be sure to communicate your wants and needs as clearly as possible, and in a way that communicates both a degree of certainty as well as an opportunity to further Protect & Serve. For example, don't say "Honey, are you and Baby OK? I want to run out to the hardware store for a bit." You are missing left here by essentially asking her for permission like all those dudes in Wimpytown need to do. Don't miss right either like those guys over in Jerkville by just rolling up to her and saying "I'm headed out to the hardware store. I'll be back later." as you head out the door.

Instead, shoot for something like the following "I'm going to the hardware store here shortly so I can get some things for my garage project, what can I help you do before I leave so that you and Baby are all set?" Notice you aren't asking for permission, yet you aren't just leaving her hanging either. You are clearly telling her your intentions to go out but are also showing her that you want to help her get what she needs before you do so. Win, win, *$ka-ching$!* You could even increase your credits earned by adding "Can I bring you a latte from the coffee shop on my way back?" Lots of ways to win here. Be creative, and start small if this all feels a little risky.

2) Plan ahead, and be specific. You might have had a long-running habit of spontaneous outings with your buddies, and Mama too for that matter. A random phone call on a Saturday morning asking you to join the pick-up basketball game that was coming together was usually an enthusiastic "Yes!" Not anymore. At least not out of the blue. You're going to have better success by setting these things up in advance, even if that requires you taking the lead with your buddies and being the one to get the game plan into place. Instead of answering that phone call on Sat morning and being thrown into a complex algorithm of how to say yes and not unexpectedly leave Mama to manage Baby by herself, you can instead tell her on Thursday that you're planning on playing basketball with your buddies from 11 – 1 on Saturday so you'd like to do brunch with her and Baby early enough to make that happen.

Here's the trick to these situations - It all comes out to how well you communicate and plan ahead so that you can find the best way to create win-win scenarios for everybody. From your side of things, you are making a decision about something that puts you and your actions at the center, and you are clearly and cleanly communicating that to Mama. You are keeping your Man Card by still living parts your life as your own person with your own interests, wants, and needs.

You're still seeing your friends, you're still making your own decisions, and you're still "you." However, from her perspective you are clearly putting your family first by looking to help get Mama and Baby set up on their own for the time you are gone. You get "I'm taking care of me," and she gets "He's putting his family first." See, how easy is that? Win, win, *$ka-ching$!*

Chapter 7 Summary for You: The 4th Trimester covers the first 3 months back home with Baby, and is an intense time of huge adjustments for everybody in every area of their lives. You, Mama, and Baby are all trying to figure out a lot of new things right now, so this chapter was focused on helping you identify common challenges faced by most Dads and then giving you the tools to make them flow easier. **Protect & Serve** is the new Dad's mantra here, everything now falls under that heading. We talked about Baby's growth chart percentiles in **D21 (Growth Chart)** and warned you about the unnecessary silliness of "competitive parenting" conversations. **D22 (Don't Take It Personally)** asked you to take a deep breath and just let Mama have some space for the emotional volatility that comes with being a new Mama. Remember, it's probably not personal and probably not something you need to "fix."

We got into the perils and dangers of Post-Partum Depression (PPD) in **B11 (PPD is Real)**, and emphasized the severity of this condition and your role in helping Mama get professional help if she starts to show symptoms by giving it some extra emphasis as **Scary Moment #4**. We talked about countering PPD and helping Mama and Baby enjoy their "Babymoon" with the simple directive to "Lavish Sisterhood, Limit Stuff," and gave you some good tips on how to help that process along. In **B12 (Own Your Role)** we discussed you fully owning your new role and responsibilities as Dad, and had a two-part conversation about the power of Baby crying in **B13 (Crying Baby)**. The first part was **Scary Moment #5,** the last one in this book, and talked about how Baby's crying can lead to moments of extreme rage in men. We told you as clear as fucking possible to **NEVER SHAKE YOUR BABY** and how doing so will completely ruin your life, Mama's life, and Baby's life. Part 2 of the power of a crying baby covered how Mamas usually respond to that sound, and **D23 (Dad Tools for Crying)** gave you some tips and strategies for being able to be the best Dad possible in those trying moments, including the womb-mimicking 5 S's of Swaddle, Side/Stomach, Shush, Swing, and Suck.

D24 (Just Do It) reminded you that besides breastfeeding, everything Baby-related is your responsibility too – just jump in and do it. Going back to work brings in another level of stress for most Dads, so **D25 (New Dad Blues Busters)** gave you some specific tips to make that daily transition easier on you and your family. Coming back to Protect & Serve, keep an eye out for those energies coming up in more intense ways than is actually helpful or necessary in most modern-day situations, as discussed in **D26 (Protect & Serve Limits)**. No punching old ladies, no matter what they might say. **D27 (Fathers Don't Mother)** covered the idea that "Fathers don't Mother," make sure Mama is on board with this one so you can both avoid silly fights about doing things "the right way." Finally, **D28 (Dad Zone Maintenance)** gave you some simple reminders to help you stay in the Dad Zone and keep your sanity. We again warned you about the Dud Zones of Wimpytown and Jerkville from **B3 (Dad Zone)** and talked about keeping both your Dad Card and Man Card fully loaded with credits by seeking ways to find win, win, *$ka-ching$* as your main goal from here on out.

Congratulations, you've made it all the way from "We're Pregnant!" through Labor & Delivery and now back home again with Baby. Hopefully you've enjoyed the journey as much as possible, and hopefully ***WTF*** and its **Big Ideas**, **Dad Tips**, and **Scary Moments** assistance have made that journey a bit easier for you, for Mama, and for Baby too. This has been a truly transformative adventure for you all, and it's my distinct pleasure to officially say "Welcome to Fatherhood!"

Chapter 7 Summary for Mama: Coming home with your new baby is a very challenging time for everybody, but more so for you Mama. So many emotions, worries, responsibilities, and feelings all coming at and through you. It can be quite overwhelming. Thankfully the bigger birth community has finally started to recognize the special challenges of this time. In fact, they have coined the term of "4th Trimester" to help connect this time more closely to the overall arc of your pregnancy and childbirth. We coached Dad here on how to best *Protect & Serve* the whole family during this 4th Trimester, specifically focusing on trying to balance his existing work and life responsibilities with all the new ones that come with having a new Baby and new Mama at home too.

We asked him to completely jump right in with any and everything that is going on, but he'll likely have no idea what to do or how to do it. As we asked you before, continue to try to be patient with him and ask him for specific things when and as you need them. Show him how you prefer certain things done, yet give him plenty of leeway to figure out how to do things his own way. At the end of the day, try not to worry about it if he isn't doing something "right" unless it is a legitimate Baby safety issue. Just like for you, this is all new for him, and remember the phrase "Fathers don't Mother." Give him room to discover his own rhythms and routines here. You both are trying to figure out this whole being a new parent thing, it's easier for everybody when you try to do it together and don't get bogged down arguing about non-essential things.

We also specifically warned Dad about the power of a crying baby. While your main feeling response to that sound may be anxiety, for many men it is anger. Therefore, we reiterated to him that it's OK to try different coping strategies to help him manage any anger that's triggered by it, and gave him some specific tips and tricks to help him try to comfort Baby in those moments. Anger at the crying is OK, but any aggression towards Baby is absolutely NOT. All in all, we encouraged him to understand the importance of looking at this 4th Trimester as a limited time that requires him to dig deep and go all out, and all in, on figuring out everything he can about what he needs to do to Protect & Serve his new family. Do what you can to help him here too. Soon enough all 3 of you will have settled into some simple routines that you have discovered and built along the way and will all be happily getting more comfortable with your new life as a complete family.

This has been one amazing adventure for you, and for him too. From "We're Pregnant" through all the ups and downs and ins and outs of your pregnancy journey. From the first pangs of labor to the overwhelming joy of finally meeting and holding Baby. From the first step off the curb when you left the birthplace to that comforting feeling of your house turning into a home as you, Dad, and Baby all settle in to some routines that work for your family. Congratulations Mama!

Epilogue

A New Hope

Sometime around or after the 3-month mark you might wake up one day and have a small yet powerful "moment of clarity." This mild epiphany will feel much like a mellower and softer version of when your eyes finally adjust to a bright light, when a loud sound source suddenly fades away, or when you realize that that a headache-induced brain fog has finally lifted. This moment is when your feet have found their balance in your new land – the land of Fatherhood.

The pregnancy journey was the slow and steady tick-tick-ticking of the rollercoaster working its way up to the top of the first hill. The labor and delivery of Baby was that first massive steep drop off the top. The first three month stretch at home was the initial stomach-churning, high speed triple loop. Now though, even with a lifetime of loops and dips and highs and lows in front of you, you feel more "settled in" and ready for what comes next than at any point in the adventure so far. You are *better connected* with Mama more than ever, and even *better prepared* for the path ahead too.

You are now a fully credited member of the Dad Zone, with all the rights, privileges, and responsibilities that come with it.

So, I'll say it one more final time, with a hearty cheer – "Welcome To Fatherhood!"

Please feel free to contact me at david@welcometofatherhood.com with any comments, questions, concerns, or suggestions that you think might help future readers of ***Welcome To Fatherhood***. I'll try to either answer your email directly or address the topic in one of my weekly blog posts that feature and focus on input from my readers. Also, if you enjoyed the book and found it helpful then please go online and leave it a positive review so that other new Dads-to-be might more easily find ***WTF*** when they are looking for guidance on their own journeys from Bump to Baby and beyond.

Thanks, and best wishes,
David Arrell
Colorado, 2020

Appendix A
Big Ideas

B1. Instant Mama - Pregnancy turns your lady into an instant Mama.
B2. Different World - It's a radically different world today for pregnancy, childbirth, and baby-rearing.
B3. Dad Zone - Dude Zone to Dad Zone, and avoiding the Dud Zones.
B4. Biggest Deal – Her becoming pregnant is the BIGGEST DEAL EVER IN HER WHOLE LIFE up to this point.
B5. Anxiety – Mama may be feeling, and expressing, a ton of ANXIETY right now.
B6. Mom Comms - Mom Comms and the Love Languages in action.
B7. Birth Space – Understanding the Birth Space concept will *greatly* improve your experience of the next 9 months, and Mama's too.
B8. Teamwork – Understand the crucial difference between "teaming up" and "teaming out."
B9. Birth Story – The Birth Story is going to be the biggest narrative in your and Mama's lives for a *long* time.
B10. New Mantra – Your mantra here is Be Attentive, Be Calm, Be Competent.
B11. PPD is Real - Post-Partum Depression is real, and a real danger to all involved.
B12. Own Your Role – Own your role as Dad, and *everything* that comes with it.
B13. Crying Baby – The power of a crying baby, parts 1 and 2.

Appendix B
Dad Tips

D1. Big 4 Ideas - Keep the above mentioned Big Ideas in mind *at all times* as you chart your course forward.
D2. Weeks - Know how many weeks pregnant she is *at all times*.
D3. Separate - Ask Mama on the daily about how she is feeling today, and then ask her separately how Baby is doing.
D4. Not an "It" – From this point forward always refer to Baby as *he/she/they* and never *"it."*
D5. Double Credits – You get double the Dad Card credits for being the one to make suggestions on *anything* related to getting ready for Baby.
D6. Birth Class - Sign up for a Birth Class.
D7. Doula – Dude, hire a Doula!
D8. Due Date – STOP talking about "due date" and START talking about "expected arrival."
D9. Gift Tracker – Put yourself in charge of the Gift Tracker Spreadsheet.
D10. Top 10 - Top Ten Baby Registry Items (for Dads).
D11. Field Trip – Take a field trip with Mama to wherever you expect to give birth to Baby.
D12. Go Bag – Get your "Go Bag" 100% stocked and ready.
D13. Birth Plan – The Birth Plan, and related decisions – know your choices.
D14. Code Words – Figure out your Code Words for Red Light, Yellow Light, and Green Light and start practicing them now.
D15. Birth Video – Watch at least 3 hi-def 1080p "Birth Videos" with Mama, including at least one C-section.
D16. Water Breaking – Her "water breaking" is NOT AN EMERGENCY.

D17. Weird Baby – Your baby might look a little weird when they first come out, do not freak out!
D18. Cradle Hold - Know how to hold your brand-new baby!
D19. Celebrate Mama – Give Mama *all* the love right now.
D20. No Idea - You have NO IDEA what you are doing, and that's 100% OK.
D21. Growth Chart – Height, Weight, and Head Circumference are somewhat silly numbers that produce silly conversations.
D22. Don't Take It Personally – Don't take anything personally. Whatever it is, it probably isn't your fault, and it probably isn't your job to fix it.
D23. Dad Tools for Crying – Use your Dad tools to conquer the crying
D24. Just Do It – Everything. Just do it all.
D25. New Dad Blues Busters.
D26. Protect & Serve Limits – Protect & Serve, but only up to a point.
D27. Fathers don't Mother.
D28. Dad Zone Maintenance & Upkeep.

Appendix C
Sample Gift Tracker Spreadsheet (GTS)

Person	Date Received	Gift Description	Place Stored	Pic Sent?
Aunt Edna	5/12/20	Blue onesie with train on it.	Gift closet	No
Uncle Mike	5/15/20	Elephant piggy bank with $100 bill in it.	Nursery shelf (Money put in new savings account for Baby)	Yes
Michelle Richards	5/17/20	Baby All Star sneakers	Gift closet	No
Philly Billy	5/20/20	Baby Phillies t-shirt	Gift closet	No

Appendix D
Go Bag Essentials

1. Multiple paper copies of your Birth Plan
2. Extension cord and power strip
3. Laptop, charger, and headphones
4. Bluetooth speaker, charger, and playlists
5. Phone chargers x 2
6. Refillable water bottle
7. Packs of mixable instant coffee and some favorite snacks
8. Changes of clothes for you and Mama, especially comfy shoes
9. Overnight toiletries bags for you and Mama
10. Prescription meds, Ibuprofen, and aspirin
11. Comfy clothes and pajamas for you and Mama
12. Favorite pillows and blankets from home
13. Massage oil
14. Several outfits for Baby
15. Pediatrician's contact info
16. IDs and insurance cards
17. Power massager
18. Heated blanket
19. Anything else that provides physical or emotional comfort

Appendix E
Birth Plan Customization

There some good Birth Plan templates available on the ***WTF*** website for download, and many others available elsewhere online too. While the styles and formatting will vary, they should all include the following items at a minimum.

1. Your first names, and Baby's too if that has been decided, written in extra-large font at the top of the page. Doing so will help your birth team connect to you better as unique individuals in this intimate setting.
2. A short list of "approved" birth friends, such as Dad, Doula, Birth Photographer, and any people explicitly NOT approved, like Med Students or Mother-in-law, just in case.
3. Atmospheric requests, such as a warmer or cooler room, lighting preferences, machine placement, etc...
4. Pain relief preferences, including types of medications and/or more natural remedies such as massage, stretching, breathing exercises, etc...

In addition to the above basic comfort and care items, there a lot of technical medical elements for both Mama and Baby that I mention below that you should discuss and decide upon in consultation with your medical professionals. Again, reflect back to our restaurant analogy. You want to see the menu of items where you have choices to make so that you can *better connect* to Mama by working through them together, and *better prepare* for the sequence of steps that will occur in Labor & Delivery.

5. For Mama these include type and frequency of fetal monitoring, IV for fluids & Hep Lock placement, assisted water breaking, chemical contracting agents, episiotomy, use of various physical tools and techniques to help Baby along, and placental delivery assistance.
6. For Baby these include delayed cord clamping, cord blood storage, delayed testing, Baby washing and wiping, Baby medical care, and various other testing procedures.

Most Hospitals and Birth Centers will have stricter policies around some of these items more than others, so work with your birth team to come up with a plan that works best for everybody involved. Remember, the ultimate goal of all childbirth events is healthy Mama and healthy Baby, don't lose sight of the bigger picture if things don't progress exactly as requested in the Birth Plan.

Made in the USA
Thornton, CO
12/30/24 17:18:56

752b3fc8-19c9-477e-a7a7-6c5e6953b7fcR01